Silent Heroes: Resistance to
Persecution of the Jews, 1933–1945

silent heroes

memorial center

resistance to
persecution of the jews
1933–1945

Silent Heroes: Resistance to Persecution of the Jews, 1933–1945

The Nazis' assumption of power on January 30, 1933, marked the beginning of the ostracism, defamation, and disenfranchisement of the roughly 500,000 German Jews. The boycott of stores with Jewish proprietors, which began on April 1, 1933; the Nuremberg race laws of September 1935; and the pogroms of November 9, 1938: these were key stages in the persecution of Jews in Germany. More than 30,000 Jewish men were imprisoned in concentration camps following the pogroms in 1938. Laws and regulations further intensified this economic and social discrimination.

Many Jews, recognizing how dangerous life in Germany was becoming, prepared for emigration with language courses and vocational retraining. More than 300,000 Jews were able to flee Germany before the war began in the fall of 1939.

Around six million people were murdered in the course of the Nazi genocide of European Jewry that began in 1941. Most were shot or gassed to death. Among them were more than 160,000 German Jews. From October 1941 on, they were largely deported to extermination camps and other killing sites in German-occupied regions of Poland and the Soviet Union and murdered there.

About 10,000 to 12,000 German Jews tried to escape this deadly threat. Because emigration was prohibited and virtually impossible even through illegal means, the only alternative was to flee underground—with a most uncertain outcome. Those who went "underground" or "into hiding" were resisting the dictatorship. Hiding places had to be found and frequently changed. There was always the danger of being denounced or discovered. Of those who evaded deportation, presumably more than half did so in Berlin. Many did not go underground until 1943, when all the remaining Jews—who had largely been in forced labor in the armaments industry—were supposed to be deported. About 5,000 of those who went into hiding survived, more than 1,700 of them in Berlin.

The survival of Jews in hiding was usually only possible with the help of people willing to offer support. Putting themselves at risk, these "silent heroes" provided food, obtained forged identity cards, helped people escape, arranged lodgings, or hid people in their own homes. Some of the helpers offered life-saving support of their own accord. They urged Jewish friends not to let themselves be deported and promised to help them survive if they went underground. Others became rescuers when they were directly asked for support by Jews or other helpers. Ideological and political motives played as much a role as did spontaneous feelings of sympathy. These helpers were able to overcome fear for their own and their families' safety, in particular their justified fear of the Gestapo.

In the course of attempts to save Jews, networks of helpers often developed. For every Jew who went underground, up to ten, and sometimes even more, non-Jewish supporters were involved, though many rescue operations nevertheless failed. Present estimates assume a total of several tens of thousands of people who helped Jews facing persecution in Germany. There were also individual Germans in the occupied countries of Europe who took advantage of their position as soldiers or in war indus-

tries to support Jews threatened with death. In view of the mass murder of European Jewry, saving individual Jews must be seen as part of the resistance to the Nazi dictatorship.

Throughout all of Europe there were people who opposed Nazi genocide by participating in rescue actions. Most of them remained silent after the war about the help they provided, which many of them saw as a matter of course. Their efforts were acknowledged only later. The Israeli Holocaust memorial Yad Vashem has so far honored as Righteous Among the Nations more than 22,000 women and men for such aid efforts. In Germany, the Silent Heroes Memorial Center is dedicated to commemorating those who escaped the mortal threat and those who helped them.

Faith and Civil Courage

Neither the Protestant nor the Catholic Church in Germany engaged in any large-scale resistance to the persecution of the Jews after 1933. The Confessing Church, which developed as an oppositional group within the German Protestant Church, rejected the exclusion of Christians of Jewish descent, but it did not openly oppose the Nazi regime. Active solidarity with "non-Aryans" was expressed solely by individual courageous Christians of both denominations. Only the small Religious Society of Friends (Quakers) called upon their members in April 1933 to show support across the board for all victims of the Nazi regime. The International Quaker Office in Berlin administered to the needs of prisoners and became a contact for people suffering persecution who sought advice in questions of emigration and in dealing with the hardships.

Church congregations were confronted with the concerns of their members who were considered Jews according to racist Nazi ideology. The St. Raphael Society, which had been supporting Catholic emigrants since 1871, and the Caritas charity organization prepared from 1933 to 1934 to assist Catholics of Jewish descent. Organized help for the far more numerous Protestant "non-Aryan" Christians developed more slowly. After several isolated initiatives, such as that of Pastor Hermann Maas in Heidelberg, the Berlin Church Aid Office for Protestant Non-Aryans, with 22 regional offices, was opened in late 1938 under the direction of Pastor Heinrich Grüber. Through the Aid Organization of the Diocese in Berlin, founded in 1938, Margarete Sommer tended to the needs of Catholics of Jewish descent. "Grüber's Office" (the Church Aid Office) was forced to close after Heinrich Grüber was arrested in December 1940, whereas the Catholic Aid Organization continued its work until the end of the war.

Some clerics boldly spoke out against the crimes of the Nazis. In his sermon at Sunday Mass on August 3, 1941, Clemens August Graf von Galen, the bishop of Münster, condemned the Nazis' murder of the sick and the handicapped. Berlin's cathedral provost Bernhard Lichtenberg was arrested in 1941 for praying publicly for persecuted Jews. Some individuals continued to demand that the church openly protest the persecution of the Jews, albeit without success. The teacher Elisabeth Schmitz wrote memorandums in 1935 and 1936 to the Confessing Church, calling for solidarity with all Jewish victims of persecution, but they were not

1 GERTRUD LUCKNER (1900–1995), 1936   2 HERMANN MAAS (1877–1970), CA. 1937

heeded. The same was true of the efforts of Margarete Sommer, who in 1942 started sending reports to the head of the German Bishops' Conference about the aims of the deportations and the initial news of mass murder.

Even once the deportations began and contact with Jews was prohibited, there were individuals who continued to offer assistance that was at the margins of legality or clearly illegal.

Some people, such as Margarethe Lachmund, a Quaker, sent letters and packages into the camps and ghettos in the German-occupied territories. Catholic Gertrud Luckner took advantage of her position as a representative of the Freiburg archbishop to support people suffering persecution. She spent two years in the Ravensbrück concentration camp (1943–1945) for helping Jews in hiding.

BIBLIOGRAPHY Behrend-Rosenfeld, Else, and Gertrud Luckner, eds. *Lebenszeichen aus Piaski: Briefe Deportierter aus dem Distrikt Lublin 1940–1943*, with an afterword by Albrecht Goes. Munich: Biederstein, 1970. | Borgstedt, Angela. "'... zu dem Volk Israel in einer geheimnisvollen Weise hingezogen': Der Einsatz von Hermann Maas und Gertrud Luckner für verfolgte Juden." In *Widerstand gegen die Judenverfolgung*, edited by Michael Kißener, 227–259. Constance: UVK Universitätsverlag, 1996. | Borries, Achim von. "'Treue Hilfe': Die Quäkerin Margarethe Lachmund (1896–1985)." *Zeitgeschichte Regional: Mitteilungen aus Mecklenburg-Vorpommern* 3, no. 1 (July 1999): 67–72. | Gailus, Manfred, ed. *Elisabeth Schmitz und ihre Denkschrift gegen die Judenverfolgung: Konturen einer vergessenen Biographie (1893–1977)*. Berlin: Wichern, 2008. | Gerlach, Wolfgang. *And the Witnesses Were Silent: The Confessing Church and the Persecution of the Jews*. Rev. ed. Edited and translated by Victoria J. Barnett. Lincoln: University of Nebraska Press, 2000. | Kuropka, Joachim, ed. *Bischof Clemens August Graf von Galen: Menschenrechte – Widerstand – Euthanasie – Neubeginn*, with the collaboration of Gian Luigi Falchi et al. Münster: Regensberg, 1998. | Leichsenring, Jana. *Die Katholische Kirche und "ihre Juden": Das "Hilfswerk beim Bischöflichen Ordinariat Berlin" 1938–1945*. Berlin: Metropol, 2007. | Ludwig, Hartmut. *An der Seite der Entrechteten und Schwachen: Zur Geschichte des "Büros Pfarrer Grüber" (1938 bis 1940) und der Ev. Hilfsstelle für ehemals Rasseverfolgte nach 1945*. Edited by Evangelische Hilfsstelle für ehemals Rasseverfolgte. Berlin: Logos, 2009. | Ogiermann, Otto. *Bis zum letzten Atemzug: Das Leben und Aufbegehren des Priesters Bernhard Lichtenberg*. Leipzig: St. Benno, 1983. | Wollasch, Hans-Josef. *Gertrud Luckner: "Botschafterin der Menschlichkeit."* Freiburg: Herder, 2005.

With Forged Documents

Gerd Ramm was a businessman with German national leanings. In the 1930s he bought several companies in Berlin and northern Germany—in part from Jews who had fled Germany—and became wealthy. In Berlin he manufactured paper and blackout equipment, which was vital for the war effort. There were some Jews doing forced labor in his workshops in Berlin-Prenzlauer Berg, but Ramm was nevertheless an undeviating opponent of the Nazi persecution of the Jews. When the forced workers were threatened with a raid, Ramm warned them and offered places to hide. Konrad Friedländer thus survived underground for three years with Ramm's help. Ramm also protected Konrad's father, Bernhard Friedländer, as well as Alfred Boehm, a Jewish dry goods businessman, and Heinz Jacobius, a young man who had been hiding from the Gestapo since 1941. Ramm hid them and others in his company and in his apartment in Berlin-Charlottenburg, which he shared with his wife and young daughter. Werner Gerth, a friend of Ramm, also provided constant support.

Ramm spent part of his fortune to obtain forged identity papers for the people he was hiding. Like most Jews who went underground in Germany, the Jews helped by Ramm did not spend all their time in hiding places, but instead tried to feign a "normal" identity under an assumed name. In order to do so they needed the appropriate identity papers. Men were at greater risk than women of being discovered in a spontaneous ID check, as the military police were constantly searching for possible deserters.

Many people who went underground tried to acquire a postal ID card. This document with a passport photograph was used as identification for picking up registered and special mail deliveries and also was recognized outside the post office as proof of identity. A permanent residence had to be listed on it. Ramm arranged for Alfred Boehm to receive a postal ID card as "Albert Schmidt," registered under Ramm's address.

Postal ID cards did not stand up to strict identity checks. Other documents were sold on the black market; for particularly high prices one could obtain forged Wehrmacht ID papers. Those whom Ramm was helping made contact with a bribable office worker in the Wehrmacht High Command (OKW). For 6,000 reichsmarks each (about 30,000 euros), this person issued identity cards for supposed civilian OKW employees to unauthorized

GERD RAMM (1906–1968), 1955

people and renewed them as needed. Heinz Jacobius disguised himself with such an ID card and arranged for Konrad Friedländer to get one as well. Ramm paid the necessary bribes for both of them. For his identity card, Konrad Friedländer used his own photograph and the personal data of his Gentile friend Rudolf Kopp. Kopp had already given him other documents of his and agreed to let Friedländer use these ID cards to apply for additional papers under the name of Rudolf Kopp.

Heinz Jacobius was arrested in late 1944 and deported to the Theresienstadt ghetto, where he survived. The other men survived the Nazi period in Berlin. Gerd Ramm saved at least ten people, for which he received the Order of Merit of the Federal Republic of Germany in 1959. Ramm was honored posthumously in May 2009 by the Israeli Holocaust memorial Yad Vashem as Righteous Among the Nations.

FORGED ID CARD OF KONRAD FRIEDLÄNDER AS "RUDOLF KOPP," AN ALLEGED CIVILIAN EMPLOYEE OF THE WEHRMACHT

Oberkommando der Wehrmacht

Dienstausweis Nr. 9 8 4 1

K o p p,   Rudolf
Name   Vorname

geboren am: 18. 12.192o zu: Berlin
Wohnort: Bln., S.W. 68, Annenstr. 5
Gestalt: mittel Gesicht: oval Haar: dkl.blond
Augen: braun Bes. Kennzeichen: keine
(O.K.W. Zivil)

Berlin, den   10. April 1943

Oberkommando der Wehrmacht

Unterschrift des Dienststellenleiters

Dienststempel

Zeitstempel

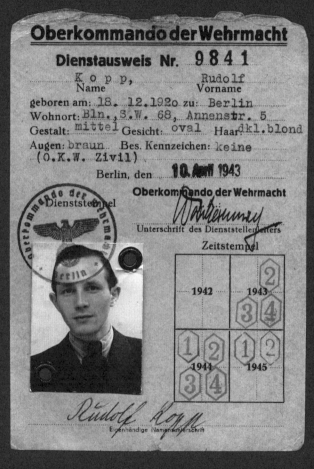

1942	1943 ②
③	④
1944 ① ②	1945 ① ②
③ ④	

Rudolf Kopp

Eigenhändige Namensunterschrift

A Network of Helpers

In July 1942, Elisabeth Abegg could do nothing to prevent her long-time close friend Anna Hirschberg, a Christian woman of Jewish descent, from being deported from Berlin. Over sixty years of age, Hirschberg did not think she could cope with living "illegally," and did not accept Abegg's offers to hide her. Years later Elisabeth Abegg learned that Hirschberg had been murdered in Auschwitz in 1944. After her friend was deported, Abegg decided to urge as many Jews as possible to flee and offered them the necessary support.

This was not the first time that Elisabeth Abegg, a left-wing liberal democrat, resisted the regime. In 1933 she was a teacher at the Berlin Luisen-Oberlyzeum, a girls' secondary school with social-democrat leanings. Along with some fellow teachers and older students, she opposed the Nazi measures at the school and the discrimination against Jewish students. Consequently, she was transferred to another school in Berlin on disciplinary grounds, where she was denounced for making remarks critical of the regime and forced into early retirement in 1941. Around that time she joined the Religious Society of Friends (Quakers), which professes nonviolence and active charity.

Abegg's oppositional group remained active even after their time together at the school. At the home of Richard Linde, the father of one of the dissident students, Abegg and others listened to BBC radio programs, from which they learned beginning in 1942 about the German crimes in the occupied territories. This knowledge reinforced their resolve to save at least individual people suffering persecution.

One of the first to find protection at Abegg's home was Liselotte Pereles, a Jewish daycare teacher who together with her foster daughter Susanne Manasse escaped deportation in February 1943. Abegg and her sister Julie secretly took them into their three-room apartment in Berlin-Tempelhof. Others who helped the two refugees were Elisabeth Schmitz, Abegg's former coworker, Hildegard Knies and Lydia Forsström, former students of Abegg, as well as Bertha Becker, a Gentile relative of Manasse. At the same time, Knies and her aunt Christine Engler attempted to save the Jewish couple Herta and Ernst Goldstein and their daughter Evelyn. Abegg's friends also helped Steffy and Ludwig Collm and their six-year-old daughter Susanne. Richard Linde took several people into his large house. The number of those

ELISABETH ABEGG (FAR RIGHT; 1882–1974) WITH LISELOTTE PERELES (FAR LEFT) IN BERLIN, 1946 seeking assistance continued to grow. Everyone involved tried to recruit additional helpers. Quarters were also found outside Berlin, such as with Frieda and Adolf Bunke in East Prussia and the seamstress Margrit Dobbeck in Alsace.

By 1945 the Abeggs had taken in twelve people who had gone underground. Some children in hiding were secretly given school instruction. All told, Elisabeth Abegg and her friends helped far more people. Through this network, an estimated eighty people were given illegal lodgings and were supported with food, money, clothing, and forged documents. Most of them survived.

Elisabeth Abegg, Hildegard Arnold-Knies, and Lydia Forsström were honored by the Israeli Holocaust memorial Yad Vashem as Righteous Among the Nations.

BIBLIOGRAPHY Pereles, Liselotte. "Die Retterin in der Not." In *Die unbesungenen Helden: Menschen in Deutschlands dunklen Tagen*, edited by Kurt R. Grossmann, 85–93. 2nd rev. ed. Frankfurt: Ullstein, 1984. | Voigt, Martina. "Grüße von 'Ferdinand': Elisabeth Abeggs vielfältige Hilfe für Verfolgte." In *Sie blieben unsichtbar: Zeugnisse aus den Jahren 1941 bis 1945*, edited by Beate Kosmala and Claudia Schoppmann, 104–116. Berlin: Förderverein Blindes Vertrauen, 2006.

HILDEGARD KNIES (1915–1997) WITH EVELYN GOLDSTEIN (B. 1938), WHO WAS SAVED, IN THE SUMMER OF 1949 IN BERLIN

Ask for "Tegel"

In April 1933, the theologian Harald Poelchau assumed the position of chaplain in the Berlin-Tegel prison. From the very beginning he was a staunch opponent of the Nazi regime and later a member of the Kreisau Circle. When deportations started in 1941 he helped Jews go underground by referring them to places to stay within his wide circle of friends and acquaintances. His wife Dorothee stood tirelessly at his side, and his long-term friend Gertie Siemsen also provided surreptitious assistance.

When Jews in hiding wanted to contact him, they were supposed to call his office in Tegel prison, but only speak if he answered the phone by saying the innocuous codeword "Tegel." Important information was discussed not on the phone, however, but in person in his office. He gave the frightened people appointments during office hours; the gatekeeper, who had a list of registered appointments, led them through numerous locked gates. In Poelchau's office they could talk freely. He referred them to reliable friends and acquaintances who were not themselves at risk.

In March 1943, the Latte family of Breslau contacted Poelchau after they went into hiding. He found lodgings for Manfred Latte with a former political prisoner and for Latte's wife Margarete with a pastor's widow, and he recommended that the son Konrad Latte contact the organist of the Berlin-Wedding crematorium. Through Konrad Latte, Poelchau met the journalist Ruth Andreas-Friedrich, an active opponent of the regime, and the two of them started working together to help Jews in hiding.

When Poelchau heard about the siblings Ralph and Rita Neumann, who had been living in hiding with Agnes Wendland, a pastor's wife, since mid-1943, he offered Ralph Neumann a job as a bicycle messenger. Ralph and Rita were arrested in February 1945, but they managed to escape from the pre-deportation camp in late March 1945 and made their way to Harald Poelchau and to safety.

After Leontine Cohn and her daughter Rita went into hiding in the Poelchau home following the Factory Action on February 27, 1943, Willi Kranz said he and his life partner Auguste Leißner were willing to take in the nine-year-old Rita. Willi Kranz ran the cafeterias in the Berlin prisons in Tegel and Plötzensee. Poelchau had known him for a long time and respected him as a "silent guardian of humanity." On numerous occasions Kranz and

HARALD POELCHAU (1903–1972), CA. 1940

Leißner also took in Konrad Latte, feeding him and recommending other reliable helpers to whom he could turn.

The twelve-year-old Jewish girl Evelyne Schwarz needed a safe hiding place in the summer of 1944. Poelchau brought her to friends, the social worker Hildegard Schneider and the progressive educator Hans-Reinhold Schneider in Berlin-Heiligensee, where she stayed for six months.

Edith Bruck, a dry nurse who had gone into hiding, heard of Harald Poelchau through her friend Hilde Benjamin. Living under a false name, she was able to take care of the house of his friends Yvonne and Peter Knoblauch, in Berlin-Grunewald. When she was arrested there, Poelchau warned her other helper, Kurt Günter Hess, who was active in the communist underground.

By the time the war ended, Harald Poelchau had helped a great number of people who had gone into hiding. Despite his membership in the Kreisau Circle, his assistance to political prisoners, and his support of "illegal" Jews, he was never interrogated or arrested by the Gestapo.

BIBLIOGRAPHY Harpprecht, Klaus. *Harald Poelchau: Ein Leben im Widerstand*. Reinbek, Germany: Rowohlt, 2004. | Poelchau, Harald. *Die Ordnung der Bedrängten: Erinnerungen des Gefängnisseelsorgers und Sozialpfarrers (1903–1972)*. Teetz, Germany: Hentrich & Hentrich, 2004. | Schneider, Peter. *"Und wenn wir nur eine Stunde gewinnen …": Wie ein jüdischer Musiker die Nazi-Jahre überlebte*. Berlin: Rowohlt, 2001. | Schneider, Peter. "Saving Konrad Latte." Translated by Leigh Hafrey. *New York Times*, February 13, 2000. http://www.nytimes.com/2000/02/13/magazine/saving-konrad-latte.html?sec=&spon=&pagewanted=1. | Schuppener, Henriette. *"Nichts war umsonst"—Harald Poelchau und der deutsche Widerstand*. Schriftenreihe der Forschungsgemeinschaft 20. Juli (July 20th Research Group Series) 7. Berlin: Lit, 2006.

HANS-REINHOLD SCHNEIDER (1897–1987) WITH HIS CHILDREN GESINE (IN HIS ARMS) AND JENS, SUMMER 1943

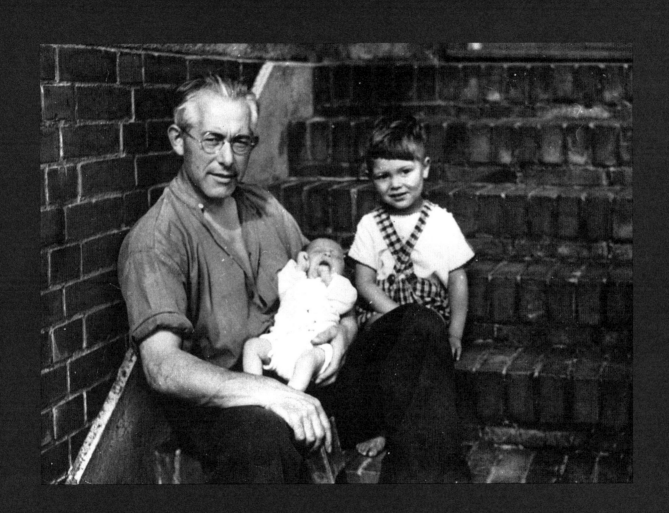

European Union

Physical chemist Robert Havemann and Dr. Georg Groscurth, later senior physician at the Robert Koch Hospital in Berlin-Moabit, became friends in 1933. Both opposed the Nazi regime from the outset. On July 15, 1943, together with Paul Rentsch and Herbert Richter, they founded the European Union resistance group in Berlin. Their long-term aim was to create "a socialist order in a united Europe." As of 1942 they also helped Jews in hiding evade deportation. Havemann arranged lodgings and procured forged ID documents. When Heinz Günther Wolff went underground with his mother in January 1943, Havemann and Groscurth arranged for both of them to hide with Hanna Stappenbeck in Schönwalde near Berlin.

Jewish businessman Walter Caro, who was living in hiding, went to the office hours of Dr. Georg Groscurth, his former doctor, in the spring of 1943 and offered forged Wehrmacht ID cards and other documents for the doctor to pass on to Jews in hiding. In the summer of 1943, Frankfurt commercial artist Walter von Scheven asked his Berlin friends to help his Jewish wife Elisabeth, as in Frankfurt even Jews living in mixed marriages were being deported. Groscurth and his wife Dr. Anneliese Groscurth, parents of two sons, a two-year-old and a two-month-old infant, harbored the Frankfurt woman in their apartment in Charlottenburg.

A dental practitioner, Paul Rentsch, and his wife Margarete, also parents of two children, helped as well. Rentsch was able to get forged ID papers for Hertha Brasch, a Jewish widow, with which she was able to hide for seven months with a seamstress in Berlin-Weissensee. The Rentsches also let Elisabeth von Scheven stay in their weekend house in the Brandenburg town of Diensdorf. Architect Herbert Richter, father of a two-year-old boy, took in Alfred and Marie Michalowitz, who had gone underground.

The members of the European Union also had contact with forced workers and prisoners of war. After only a short time, however, the resistance group was discovered, and Havemann, the Groscurths, and Richter and his wife Maria were arrested. When Paul and Margarete Rentsch were arrested in Diensdorf, Elisabeth von Scheven was also discovered.

Because the wives were not convicted of any political activities, they were released and could return to their children in De-

1 ROBERT HAVEMANN (1910–1982), CA. 1940 2 ELISABETH VON SCHEVEN (1906–2000) AFTER HER ARREST IN SEPTEMBER 1944

cember 1943. On May 8, 1944, Georg Groscurth, Herbert Richter, and Paul Rentsch were executed in the Brandenburg-Görden penitentiary. In his last letter to his wife, Groscurth wrote, "Remember that we are dying for a better future, for a life without hatred. […] I die proud and unbroken."

Robert Havemann was also sentenced to death. However, friends arranged a research job for him that was ostensibly vital to the war effort, and he survived the war in prison.

Hertha Brasch, Agnes Wolff, and her son Heinz Günther were deported to Auschwitz in early 1944 and murdered there. Walter Caro died in Auschwitz in March 1945, two months after liberation. Elisabeth von Scheven survived the Auschwitz concentration camp, the only survivor among those helped by the group.

In 2005 the Israeli Holocaust memorial Yad Vashem honored Anneliese and Georg Groscurth, Robert Havemann, Paul Rentsch, and Herbert Richter as Righteous Among the Nations.

BIBLIOGRAPHY Florath, Bernd. "Die Europäische Union." In "Der vergessene Widerstand"—Zu Realgeschichte und Wahrnehmung von Opposition und Widerstand gegen den Nationalsozialismus, edited by Johannes Tuchel, 114–139. Göttingen: Wallstein, 2005. | Hannemann, Simone. Robert Havemann und die Widerstandsgruppe "Europäische Union." Berlin: Robert-Havemann-Gesellschaft, 2001. | Sandvoß, Hans-Rainer. "Deutsche und Ausländer (Zwangsarbeiter) im Widerstand: Europäische Union." In Die "andere" Reichshauptstadt: Widerstand aus der Arbeiterbewegung in Berlin 1933 bis 1945, 241–254. Berlin: Lukas, 2007.

THE ENGAGED COUPLE ANNELIESE PLUMPE (1910–1996) AND GEORG GROSCURTH (1904–1944) IN 1938

From Parsonage to Parsonage

Born in 1888, Max Krakauer was running a major film distribution company as of 1918 in Leipzig, where he met his wife Karoline ("Ines") Rosenthal. The Jewish businessman was forced to sell his company after 1933, and subsequently worked at a poorly paid job as a travel representative. In 1939 the Krakauers moved to Berlin, where their plans to emigrate failed. Only their daughter Inge made it to England in 1939.

The Krakauers were in forced labor when, on January 29, 1943, they barely escaped deportation. Desperate, they contacted an acquaintance, Hans Ackermann, a Protestant Christian who brought them to Wilhelm Jannasch, a pastor who was active in the Confessing Church. Jannasch advised them to hide in rural Pomerania, as many Jews had already gone underground in Berlin. He referred them to parsonages of the Confessing Church there. Ackermann gave them his expired postal ID card and replaced his photograph with Max Krakauer's. He drew in the missing part of the stamp. The Krakauers used this primitively forged ID card to embark on a risky journey on March 9, 1943, at a time when ID documents were often checked on trains. After they had gone through all possible lodgings in Pomerania, they returned to Berlin in the summer of 1943.

Pastor Theodor Burckhardt later referred the Krakauers to Kurt Müller, a pastor in Stuttgart. In 1943, Müller set up a support network together with other clerics of the Protestant state church who sympathized with the Confessing Church. More than forty pastors' families and people they trusted formed this "parsonage chain" in Württemberg, which succeeded in saving roughly thirteen Jews. Some of the participating clerics were already being observed by the Gestapo because of their critical views, including Theodor Dipper of Reichenbach, Richard Gölz of Wankheim, and Otto Mörike of Flacht.

In order to minimize the risk faced by the helpers, Max and Ines Krakauer, who called themselves "Hans and Grete Ackermann," stayed for only a short time at each location. They usually were introduced as a "bombed-out couple from Berlin" and were "passed on" every few weeks or days. Their presence was somewhat less conspicuous because parsonages often had guests anyway. After more than 800 days on the run and after many separations, Ines and Max Krakauer were liberated by the U.S. Army on April 21, 1945. They remained in Stuttgart after the war.

Max (1888–1965) and Karoline "Ines" (1894–1972) Krakauer, summer 1945

The fact that they owed their survival to the courageous aid of numerous Germans facilitated their decision to stay in Germany after the war. Almost all of their relatives had been killed in con-centration camps. Max Krakauer described the different stations of their underground life in his book *Lichter im Dunkel* (Lights in the Dark), which was published in 1947.

BIBLIOGRAPHY Krakauer, Max. *Lichter im Dunkel: Flucht und Rettung eines jüdischen Ehepaares im Dritten Reich*. Rev. ed. Edited by Gerda Riehm and Jörg Thierfelder, with Susanne Fetzer. Foreword by Eberhard Röhm. Stuttgart: Calwer, 2007. | Haigis, Peter. *Sie halfen Juden: Schwäbische Pfarrhäuser im Widerstand*. Stuttgart: Evangelische Gemeindepresse, 2007.

CHURCH AND PARSONAGE (CENTER) IN GEBERSHEIM, CA. 1940

Destination: Switzerland

Luise Meier of Berlin-Grunewald empathized with her Jewish neighbors who were desperately trying to flee Germany. A devout Catholic, she opposed the Nazi regime and looked for ways to help people threatened by it. She temporarily hid a Jewish couple in her apartment and was able to help them escape to Switzerland in 1942.

When the widow Meier, born in 1885, was asked to help a Jewish woman whom she did not know, she also agreed. In the spring of 1943 she accompanied Lotte Kahle on a risky journey to Singen near Lake Constance and got to know Josef Höfler, who lived with his family in the border town of Gottmadingen. Höfler was a skilled worker at the aluminum rolling mill in Singen, so he had not been drafted. Out of compassion he was willing to help, even though it meant putting also his wife and his daughter at risk. Josef Höfler and Luise Meier agreed to continue to assist others to flee.

Luise Meier often accompanied the Jewish women and men on their trip from Berlin to Singen. Josef Höfler and his coworkers Willy Vorwalder and Wilhelm Ritzi, as well as Ritzi's cousin Hugo Wetzstein, would then bring the Jews to the irregular, difficult-to-monitor border and give the refugees explicit directions so that they could avoid border guards. The lights of the border towns in the Swiss canton of Schaffhausen also served as an orientational aid, because Switzerland, in contrast to Germany, did not black out its towns at night. It was particularly dangerous for Jewish men to escape. For the long train ride from Berlin they needed well-forged military papers that would stand up to controls by the military police looking for deserters. After a failed escape attempt in May 1944, when two Jewish women were caught by the Gestapo and then deported, all of the helpers were arrested.

In July 1944 the case was transferred from the Special Court in Freiburg to the "People's Court," where the helpers were to be charged with "aiding the enemy," for which the penalty was either death or penal servitude for life. In the chaos of the final months of the war, however, the trial never took place. After a year in prison and anxious waiting, the accused helpers were released in the spring of 1945.

Luise Meier and the other helpers were able to assist 28 Jewish men and women to Switzerland, including Lotte Kahle and her later husband Herbert Strauss. It was through their efforts

JOSEF HÖFLER (1911–1994), LUISE MEIER (1885–1979), GERTRUD (B. 1938), AND ELISE HÖFLER (1912–1991), CA. 1952

that Luise Meier and Josef Höfler were honored posthumously in
2001 by the Israeli Holocaust memorial Yad Vashem as Righteous
Among the Nations.

BIBLIOGRAPHY Battel, Franco. "Ein Netz von Helferinnen und Helfern: Die Fluchthilfe um Luise Meier und Josef Höfler." In *"Wo es hell ist, dort ist die Schweiz." Flüchtlinge und Fluchthilfe an der Schaffhauser Grenze zur Zeit des Nationalsozialismus*, 204–215. Zurich: Chronos, 2000. | Schoppmann, Claudia. "Fluchtziel Schweiz: Das Hilfsnetz um Luise Meier und Josef Höfler." In *Überleben im Dritten Reich: Juden im Untergrund und ihre Helfer*, edited by Wolfgang Benz, 205–219. Munich: C. H. Beck, 2003.

LOTTE KAHLE (B. 1911), LATER LOTTE STRAUSS, AFTER HER ESCAPE TO SWITZERLAND, 1943

Help for an Escapee from Majdanek

Robert Eisenstädt, a young technician from Hanau, wanted to go into hiding in 1942 to avoid deportation. He had already been imprisoned in the Buchenwald concentration camp after the November Pogrom in 1938. However, when his family received its notice to report for deportation, his non-Jewish friends who were going to take him in became frightened at the last minute and took back their offer of lodgings. On May 30, 1942, Eisenstädt, his mother, five siblings, and his young nephew were deported to Lublin, in Poland.

A few weeks later Eisenstädt escaped from the Majdanek concentration camp and fled to Frankfurt via Radom and Bres-lau. He was hidden by his Jewish fiancée Eva Müller in Frankfurt and also by friends in Hanau. Hans Waider, the boyfriend of Eisenstädt's sister Martha and the father of her son, was a soldier in the German Air Force (Luftwaffe). When he was home on leave in late 1942 he learned from Robert Eisenstädt that Martha and the boy had been deported. The despairing soldier at least wanted to help his girlfriend's brother. He gave him his boots and stole the ID card of a civilian employee from a Hanau office of the Wehrmacht; Eisenstädt's photo was inserted into it.

Eva Müller was expecting a child with Robert Eisenstädt. A trained corsetiere, she and her family had moved from Czechoslovakia to Frankfurt in the late 1920s. As a foreign Jew she was spared deportation for the time being. She had stayed in contact with her physician in Frankfurt, Dr. Fritz Kahl, and his wife Margarete, and turned to them to ask for help. Dr. Kahl and his wife, parents of four children, took in Robert Eisenstädt for several weeks. They arranged to get forged ID papers and worked together with others to help the couple escape to Switzerland.

Kahl's sixteen-year-old son Eugen was assigned Luftwaffe support outside the city with his class at school. When he came home unexpectedly, his parents told him they were hiding a Jew in their home. He had to keep this news absolutely secret and not tell his friends.

Eva Müller and Robert Eisenstädt succeeded in escaping across the border to Switzerland on February 21, 1943. While climbing over the barbed-wire fence the pregnant woman injured her legs. Eisenstädt had been seriously abused in the concentration camp and recovered only slowly from his injuries and

ROBERT EISENSTÄDT (1919–1996), CA. 1946

the ordeal of the escape. Their daughter Maria Adyna Eisenstädt (called Maja) was born on July 8, 1943, in Basel.

Eva Müller's sister Berta had remained in Frankfurt. In March 1943 she was ordered to report to the Gestapo for deportation. At the last moment she too asked Dr. Kahl for help. Margarete and Fritz Kahl hid Berta Müller for several weeks in their home.

Dr. Kahl procured a forged ID card, with which she escaped to Vienna. There she was able to live anonymously, albeit at great risk.

In 2006 the Israeli Holocaust memorial Yad Vashem honored Fritz and Margarete Kahl posthumously as Righteous Among the Nations.

BIBLIOGRAPHY Kosmala, Beate. "Robert Eisenstädts Flucht aus dem KZ Majdanek: Über Frankfurt am Main in die Schweiz." In *Überleben im Dritten Reich: Juden im Untergrund und ihre Helfer*, edited by Wolfgang Benz, 113–130. Munich: C. H. Beck, 2003. | Kosmala, Beate, and Revital Ludewig-Kedmi. "Rettung eines Flüchtlings aus Majdanek: Margarete und Fritz Kahl." In *Verbotene Hilfe: Deutsche Retterinnen und Retter während des Holocaust*, edited by Beate Kosmala and Revital Ludewig-Kedmi, with a foreword by Emil Walter-Busch, 43–49. Zurich: Pestalozzianum, 2003.

MARGARETE KAHL (1896–1958) AND FRITZ KAHL (1895–1974) WITH THEIR SONS, AFTER 1945

A Rescuer in Uniform

Karl Plagge, a chemical engineer from Darmstadt, had joined the Nazi Party in 1931, but by 1938 at the latest he distanced himself from Nazism. After the Soviet Union was invaded, the 44-year-old Plagge, a captain in the Wehrmacht, was transferred on July 1, 1941, to Vilnius, Lithuania, to set up and direct an army motor transport park (HKP).

In Vilnius, Plagge witnessed mass executions of Jews and the ghettoization of the Jewish population there under the brutal German occupation regime. He tried to treat the Jewish forced laborers humanely, which made HKP jobs sought-after by those in the ghetto.

Before the ghetto was liquidated in the fall of 1943, Plagge, now a major, managed to obtain authorization from the SS leadership to set up a separate work camp outside the ghetto for his forced laborers. At night in mid-September of 1943, he drove with trucks to the gate of the ghetto and had a large number of HKP workers with their wives and children picked up and moved to the new camp, which comprised two large, multilevel residential blocks. More than one thousand people could be moved to the HKP camp. Plagge remained camp commandant until early July 1944; he tried to protect the work camp inmates from SS terror as best he could and to give them sufficient food. The massiveness of the building facilitated the construction of hideouts, which many people later used to save themselves.

Ida and Samuel Esterowicz and their daughter Perela (later Pearl Good) were among the survivors who viewed Karl Plagge as their rescuer. On September 6, 1941, the Germans forced them to move into the Vilnius ghetto, where they lived in claustrophobic conditions. The parents experienced a blessing in disguise: as forced laborers in the HKP, they were among those moved to Plagge's work camp. Working feverishly at night, Samuel Esterowicz and other men built a hideout. Starting on July 1, 1944, the family spent days in the hideout under horrendous conditions until the Germans finally abandoned the camp.

Fifteen-year-old Simon Malkes and his father worked as electricians in the HKP. The Malkes family was also moved to the HKP work camp run by Major Plagge. Like Samuel Esterowicz, Simon's father worked nights building a hiding place. In June 1944, Plagge sent Simon's mother to a hospital, where she was able to stay until liberation. On July 1, 1944, Plagge managed to warn the camp

MAJOR KARL PLAGGE (1897–1957) IN VILNIUS, CA. 1944

inmates of the imminent arrival of the SS and the liquidation of the camp. Simon and his father went into their hiding place, and they too survived.

By the time the Red Army arrived in mid-July of 1944, more than 90 percent of the 220,000 Lithuanian Jews had been murdered under German occupation. On June 21, 1944, Plagge wrote to his wife: "Neither among my superiors nor among my subordinates is there anyone with whom I can express myself." As one of his motives for his actions, he stated, "Because I—precisely as a former National Socialist—feel responsible for everything that has happened."

Thanks to the efforts of survivors, Karl Plagge—who died in 1957—was honored posthumously in 2005 by the Israeli Holocaust memorial Yad Vashem as Righteous Among the Nations.

BIBLIOGRAPHY Good, Michael. *Searching for Major Plagge: The Nazi Who Saved Jews*. New York: Fordham University Press, 2006. | Bak, Samuel. *Painted in Words: A Memoir*. Foreword by Amos Oz. Bloomington, IN: Indiana University Press, 2001. | Viefhaus, Marianne. "Für eine Gemeinschaft der 'Einsamen unter ihren Völkern': Major Plagge und der Heereskraftfahrpark 562 in Wilna." *In Zivilcourage: Empörte, Helfer und Retter aus Wehrmacht, Polizei und SS*, edited by Wolfram Wette, 97–113. Frankfurt: Fischer Taschenbuch, 2004. | Viefhaus, Marianne. *Zivilcourage in der Zeit des Holocaust: Karl Plagge aus Darmstadt, ein "Gerechter unter den Völkern."* Edited by Darmstädter Geschichtswerkstatt and the Magistrat der Wissenschaftsstadt Darmstadt. Darmstadt: Darmstädter Geschichtswerkstatt, Magistrat der Wissenschaftsstadt Darmstadt, 2005. | Viefhaus, Marianne. *Karl Plagge (1897–1957)—the "Schindler" from Darmstadt*. Translated by Mimi Sherwin. Available at the online Plagge Document Depository: http://web.me.com/michaeldg/Site/Plagge_Documents.html.

PERELA ESTEROWICZ (B. 1929), LATER PEARL GOOD, 1947

Survival in Disguise—From Poland to Berlin

Donata and Eberhard Helmrich were married in 1933 in Berlin. Both were staunch opponents of the Nazi regime and helped their Jewish friends in many ways, such as with their plans to emigrate. In the summer of 1941, Eberhard Helmrich, an agricultural expert, was sent to the German-occupied Polish city of Drohobycz, near Lvov, to do compulsory service as the director of the food and agriculture administration. He tried to mitigate the hardship of the Jews there by smuggling food into the Drohobycz ghetto. In the spring of 1942 the Hyrawka work camp was erected on his suggestion, where fruits and vegetables were cultivated to feed the local SS. He used his influence to protect the roughly 200 Jewish women and men in "his" camp and to ensure that working and living conditions were more or less tolerable. During SS raids he hid Jews in his house. When Hyrawka was liquidated in September 1943, Helmrich helped many Jews escape.

In the fall of 1942 he made it possible for several Jewish women to escape Drohobycz by procuring forged ID papers of Christian Ukrainians for them; he had them go to his wife in Berlin. Despite her concern for her own children, Donata Helmrich took

them—including Anita Brunnengraber and Melania Reifler—into her home in Berlin-Charlottenburg. New quarters had to be arranged when neighbors became suspicious. Because many families sought inexpensive domestic help, Donata Helmrich found jobs for the young women as alleged Christian Ukrainians, who in contrast to Poles were permitted to work in German households. They first had to apply for a permit at the employment office. Then the "Ukrainians" had to undergo an official aptitude test, including head measurements. They had to be careful not to give themselves away among their supposed compatriots through their speech, and had to keep their cool during ID checks by the police. They couldn't let the German families they worked for find out who they really were.

Crafty and undaunted, Donata Helmrich also assisted Jewish acquaintances from Berlin by either hiding them or forging registration papers. She "lost" her ID card several times, each time giving it to a Jew who had gone underground, such as Herta Pineas, who wished to flee to southern Germany. "We figured that once we saved two lives, we'd be even with Hitler if we were caught, and every person saved beyond that would put us one

1 Eberhard Helmrich (1899–1969), 1948   2 Donata Helmrich (1900–1986), ca. 1946

ahead." That was Donata and Eberhard Helmrich's attitude. It is estimated that they helped between 70 and 300 Jews.

The Israeli Holocaust memorial Yad Vashem honored Eberhard Helmrich in 1965 and Donata Helmrich (posthumously) in 1986 as Righteous Among the Nations.

BIBLIOGRAPHY Schmalz-Jacobsen, Cornelia. *Zwei Bäume in Jerusalem*. Hamburg: Hoffmann und Campe, 2002.

ANITA BRUNNENGRABER (LEFT), MELANIA REIFLER, AND THE CHILDREN OF THE HAMBURG FAMILY FOR WHOM REIFLER WORKED; PHOTO TAKEN DURING THE WAR

Nazi Victims Helping the Hunted

The family of the well-known Social Democratic Party (SPD) politician and journalist Ernst Heilmann lived in Berlin-Kreuzberg. Heilmann, at the time a member of the Reichstag for the SPD, was arrested only a few days after the SPD was banned on June 22, 1933. After seven years' imprisonment, torture, and humiliation in a number of concentration camps, he was murdered on April 3, 1940, in the Buchenwald concentration camp.

Following his arrest, his wife Magdalena and their four children—Eva, Peter, Ernst Ludwig, and Beate, born between 1920 and 1927—lived under great material hardship and constant worry. As relatives of a political prisoner who also had a Jewish family background, the Heilmanns suffered discrimination on many levels. The children were disparaged at school and limited in their choice of career.

The Heilmanns, who received support from regime opponents in their large circle of friends and acquaintances, witnessed the persecution of relatives and close friends. In the knowledge of the Nazis' crimes and despite the risks posed to them, Magdalena Heilmann and her children continued to shelter people seeking protection from the Gestapo by letting them stay in their apartment at Blücherstrasse 66 in Kreuzberg. They were assisted by Social Democrats, former trade unionists, and others suffering political persecution.

Eva and Ernst Ludwig Heilmann arranged to get extra food for people in hiding. Peter Heilmann joined the Quaker youth group in Berlin. The small religious community rejected racist exclusion, so it was possible for young people of Jewish descent to find friends in the group. Peter Heilmann made contact with numerous regime opponents in order to arrange lodgings and provide forged ID papers for people in hiding.

Between 1942 and 1945 the Heilmanns provided at least temporary refuge to a number of Jews who had gone underground: their friend Else Behrend-Rosenfeld, who had escaped from Munich; Toni Kaliski-Boronow, Lotte Kahle, and Herbert Strauss; the adolescents Walter Joelson and Ernst Schwerin; and—for an extended period of time—Eva and Martin Deutschkron.

Lotte Kahle and, a short time later, Herbert Strauss were able to escape to Switzerland in the spring of 1943 with the help of the network around Luise Meier and Josef Höfler. Hella Gorn, Peter Heilmann's Gentile girlfriend from the Quaker group,

Else Behrend-Rosenfeld (right; 1891–1970) with her helpers Ernst Ludwig Heilmann (left), Hella Gorn (second from left) and Lotte and Edmund Goldschagg (center), Hinterzarten/Black Forest, winter 1943/44

maintained contact with their liaisons so that other people whom the Heilmanns protected could be rescued in this way.

Sent to a work camp in October 1944, Peter Heilmann escaped in February 1945 and went underground. Magdalena Heil- mann was interrogated by the Gestapo several times but never arrested. She, her children, and most of the people whom they protected survived the Nazi persecution.

BIBLIOGRAPHY Behrend-Rosenfeld, Else R. *Ich stand nicht allein: Leben einer Jüdin in Deutschland 1933 bis 1944*, with an afterword by Marita Krauss. Munich: C. H. Beck, 1988. | Sandvoß, Hans-Rainer. *Widerstand in Kreuzberg*. Vol. 10 of *Widerstand in Berlin von 1933 bis 1945*. Berlin: Gedenkstätte Deutscher Widerstand, 1996. See esp. 74–76, 253–255. | Strauss, Herbert A. *In the Eye of the Storm: Growing up Jewish in Germany 1918–1943, A Memoir*. New York: Fordham University Press, 1999. | Strauss, Lotte. *Over the Green Hill: A German Jewish Memoir 1913–1943*. New York: Fordham University Press, 1999. | Rathburn, Arthur and Ursula. *No More Tears Left Behind: The Remarkable Life Story of Holocaust Survivor Eva Deutschkron*. Dane, Wisc.: Fort Dane Books, 2009.

MAGDALENA HEILMANN (1894–1986), BERLIN, 1940S

Help in the Factory

Metal turner Wilhelm Daene was a Social Democrat and an active trade unionist in Thuringia until 1933. Starting in 1935 he worked in Alfred Teves's machine factory in Berlin-Wittenau, where in October 1941 he became foreman for the female Jewish forced laborers. Not only did he treat them humanely, but he used his position to mitigate their hardship. He obtained additional food for them through the factory. The company doctor also was not a Nazi and agreed to Daene's request to give the Jewish women medical treatment. Daene observed that deportations were increasing from 1942 on; he was able to retain "his" women as workers vital to the war effort so that they would not be deported. Until the Factory Action in late February 1943, his efforts were usually successful.

In 1942 he allowed one of the forced laborers, Lotte Markiewicz, to stay in a closed-off section of the production hall to recover from a nervous breakdown. That year he also protected Charlotte Josephy from being charged with making unauthorized telephone calls, which could have meant her immediate deportation. When she went into hiding, Daene kept in contact with her and helped her with important decisions. He worked out a plan to save Emilie Isaak, in which she was disguised as a Belgian civilian forced worker. Daene acquired a Belgian passport for her and made all the necessary alterations. She was able to survive in her alleged home country. Daene also helped Felix Luxenburg avoid getting picked up during the Factory Action on February 27, 1943. Luxenburg went underground and Daene stayed in contact with him as well.

Daene and his wife Margarete, who got married in 1936, hid three Jewish women in their home. They lived in Berlin-Konradshöhe in the house of Margarete's parents Ernst and Klara Rentsch, who also helped out. They had a large vegetable garden and a private poultry breeding business, which were invaluable in feeding the women in hiding. Two of the women, Ursula Finke and Lola Alexander, spent their days working under assumed names in Margarete Daene's lending libraries. In early August 1944, Finke was waylaid by a Gestapo informer at the Gesundbrunnen commuter rail station; in mortal fear she threw herself in front of an incoming train. Seriously injured, she remained in the Jewish Hospital until the end of the war.

WILHELM DAENE (1899–1981) IN ONE OF HIS WIFE'S LENDING LIBRARIES, BERLIN, CA. 1940

In August 1944 Wilhelm Daene was arrested for participating in a resistance group at the company. The two women he was still hiding, Lola Alexander and Gerda Lesser, had to quickly flee to alternative lodgings. In late August 1944, Lesser was nevertheless arrested. She was deported, first to Theresienstadt in September and later to Auschwitz, where she was murdered. Alexander returned to Margarete Daene and her work in the lending library in the fall of 1944.

Wilhelm Daene was acquitted in his trial in December 1944 before the People's Court, but his fear of the Gestapo led him to go into hiding for the rest of the war. Because of the imaginative and persistent help of Margarete and Wilhelm Daene, most of the people they hid survived.

BIBLIOGRAPHY Grossmann, Kurt R. "Ein Werkmeister erzählt." In *Die unbesungenen Helden: Menschen in Deutschlands dunklen Tagen*, 32–48. Frankfurt: Ullstein, 1984.

URSULA FINKE (LEFT) AND LOLA ALEXANDER, BERLIN, SUMMER 1945

At the Site of Mass Murder

In July 1941, when he was barely 28 years old, Berthold Beitz moved to Borysław in German-occupied Eastern Galicia to assume responsibility for the most important oil wells of the Beskidian (later Carpathian) Oil Company. As an expert in the administration of the Eastern Galician crude oil fields, which was classified as vital to the war effort, Beitz was exempted from military service.

From 1918 to 1939, Borysław and its oil fields (Polish: *nafta*) belonged to Poland; thereafter and up to June 22, 1941, it was occupied by the Soviets. Of the roughly 40,000 inhabitants of Borysław, most of whom worked in the oil industry, 18,000 were Jews; the other inhabitants were Poles and Ukrainians.

As the company's business manager, Beitz was horrified by the mass execution of Jews and, starting in the spring of 1942, the deportations that were carried out by the SS. He decided to save as many of the Jewish forced workers in his charge at the Carpathian Oil Company as possible from shootings and deportation to the Bełżec camp, even though it was not at first known that Bełżec was an extermination camp.

His wife Else Beitz, together with their one-year-old daughter Barbara, joined her husband in Borysław in Eastern Galicia. She too was shocked at the brutal persecution of Jews to which she was an eyewitness. She was her husband's only ally there. Jews often sat on their steps asking for help. Else and Berthold Beitz repeatedly hid Jews, including children, in their home when raids were about to take place.

From March to December 1942, Beitz continually managed to take his workers and others off the death trains bound for the Bełżec extermination camp. His self-assured, firm manner helped him get his way with the SS. When in October 1942 the young Zygmunt Spiegler risked losing his job in the kitchen of the forced labor camp, it was tantamount to a death sentence, as Spiegler also would have lost his "R" badge, which identified him as an armaments worker and thus saved him temporarily from deportation. Beitz transferred the sixteen-year-old to the "house administration and construction department" on paper only. Spiegler could thus retain his status as an armaments worker but continue working in the kitchen. Beitz had already brought him back from a transport on two previous occasions. Spiegler survived.

ELSE BEITZ (B. 1920) AND BERTHOLD BEITZ (B. 1913) WITH THEIR DAUGHTER BARBARA, CA. 1942 IN BORYSŁAW

Beitz was also able to save Josef Hirsch, his Jewish accounting clerk, as well as Hirsch's wife and their eight-year-old son. On the day before a major raid in Borysław in early August 1942, Hirsch asked Beitz to refrain from taking a planned trip. Beitz remained in Borysław and hid his Jewish workers in a locked room. In 1947, Hirsch wrote, "I regard Mr. Berthold Beitz as having saved my life and that of my wife and child."

An upright man, Beitz was denounced several times and almost arrested once. Before leaving Borysław upon being drafted into the Wehrmacht in April 1944, he advised the Jews to escape by fleeing into the forests until the Red Army arrived. At least 100 people survived due to his rescue efforts.

The Israeli Holocaust memorial Yad Vashem honored Berthold Beitz in 1973 and Else Beitz in 2006 as Righteous Among the Nations.

BIBLIOGRAPHY Sandkühler, Thomas. *"Endlösung" in Galizien: Der Judenmord in Ostpolen und die Rettungsinitiative von Berthold Beitz 1941–1944*. Bonn: Dietz, 1996. | Schmalhausen, Bernd. *Berthold Beitz im Dritten Reich: Mensch in unmenschlicher Zeit*. Essen: Pomp, 1991.

JOSEF HIRSCH AND HIS WIFE MARIE, CA. 1938 IN BORYSŁAW

Spontaneous Assistance

In late 1942, Maria Nickel, a mother of two young boys, saw forced workers wearing the Yellow Star near her apartment in Berlin-Kreuzberg. One of them was pregnant. A devout Catholic, Nickel spontaneously decided to help the woman. She followed the Jewish woman to the factory where she worked, and the owner let Nickel talk to her.

Ruth Abraham was surprised at first, as contact between Jews and Gentiles was illegal. Her husband Walter Abraham was also suspicious. But Maria Nickel soon appeared at the Abrahams' home with food. The women got to know each other. One day Ruth Abraham asked her new friend for help in acquiring forged identity papers. She and her husband had been planning for some time to flee once their child was born. Maria Nickel got a post office ID card made out in her own name and Ruth's photograph was inserted. She gave Walter Abraham the driver's license of her husband Willi, a truck driver.

In late January 1943, only a few days after the birth of their daughter Reha, Ruth and Walter Abraham went into hiding with their child. They paid a large sum of money for a rural address of an elderly woman near Landsberg an der Warthe (Polish: Gorzów Wielkopolski). This woman rented them a cabin, where they lived for a while without any outside assistance. One day during a police check the Abrahams presented the Nickels' ID papers, which were confiscated for verification. The Abrahams managed to escape and called Maria Nickel to warn her. They stayed in contact, and Nickel continued to help them. Although frightened, she managed to outwit the Gestapo when they interrogated her. They threatened to take away her children if they could prove that she was "aiding Jews," but they ultimately let her go. Despite this intimidation, Nickel continued to help the Jews undeterred. She frequently took in Reha, and once she arranged for the baby to be treated in a hospital under her name. Maria Nickel remained the Abrahams' most important helper.

When the Abrahams desperately sought a new hiding place in the early summer of 1943, they remembered a friendly greengrocer and his wife in Berlin-Charlottenburg, whom they had met in 1939. When Walter Abraham asked them, Bodo and Reinholde Goede spontaneously decided to take him in. The childless elderly woman treated Walter Abraham like her own son. Ruth Abraham and the baby could visit now and then. She lived with

1 MARIA NICKEL (1910–2001), EARLY 1930S IN BERLIN 2 RUTH ABRAHAM (1913–2003), CA. 1939

her daughter under a false name in Neudamm (Polish: Dębno), east of the Oder River. Despite the risk, Walter Abraham visited his family regularly and brought them money from black-market trading.

The family was together in Neudamm when the war ended. After liberation, Walter was interned in a Soviet camp. He was finally released through the perseverance of his wife. The family returned to Berlin together. They immigrated to New York in 1948. Ruth Abraham and Maria Nickel remained close friends for the rest of their lives.

Maria Nickel was honored in 1968 by the Israeli Holocaust memorial Yad Vashem as Righteous Among the Nations.

BIBLIOGRAPHY Sokolow, Reha, and Al Sokolow. *Ruth und Maria: Eine Freundschaft auf Leben und Tod (Berlin 1942–1945),* edited and with an introduction by Beate Kosmala. Berlin: Metropol, 2006. | Sokolow, Reha, and Al Sokolow, with Debra Galant. *Defying the Tide: An Account of Authentic Compassion During the Holocaust.* Englewood, NJ: Devora Publishing, 2003.

RUTH AND WALTER ABRAHAM (1906–1979) WITH THEIR DAUGHTER REHA (B. 1943) IN HIDING, CA. 1944

Fled a Death Transport

The Jewish brothers Michael and Jurek Rozenek grew up near Krakow. After the Wehrmacht occupied Poland, their family was forced into the Lodz ghetto in Poland in 1940. In August 1944, they were deported to the Auschwitz-Birkenau death camp. Their parents and most of their siblings were murdered, but the two brothers were sent to Czechowitz, a satellite camp of Auschwitz-Monowitz, where they were forced to work to total exhaustion. In late 1944, Czechowitz was hastily evacuated as the Red Army approached. The prisoners were forced by the SS to trek to Gleiwitz on foot. There a transport brought the inmates, half frozen to death, to the Buchenwald concentration camp. A few days later, in January 1945, the Rozeneks were brought to Rehmsdorf, a satellite camp of Buchenwald, where they had to do extremely hard labor under disastrous conditions.

In early April 1945, all the prisoners in Rehmsdorf were being brought to Theresienstadt in open coal freight cars, without food or water. While in the Erz Mountains, the Rozeneks managed to jump from the train and escape into the forest. There they happened to meet Arno Bach of Niederschmiedeberg on April 16. As a stoker in a paper factory, Bach had been deferred from military service. He felt compassion for the totally exhausted men, gave them something to eat, and promised he would return that evening. "We were still mistrustful, since we thought it was virtually impossible that there were still Germans who really wanted to help us," wrote Michael Rozenek in 1989 about his first encounter with the man who saved their lives.

When he got home, Bach, a Social Democrat and opponent of the Nazi regime, discussed the matter with his wife Margarete. She also wanted to help. They had recently learned that their oldest son had been killed in action and the younger one was missing. The Bachs hid the Jewish brothers in a shed behind their home. They had to be very cautious because there were Nazis living in the neighborhood. Margarete Bach would pretend that she was getting wood from the shed and bring along food in a basket that she used for garden work.

Arno Bach lived in the same house as his sister Luise Griesmann and her husband Alfred. The two of them and another neighbor Frieda Löser, a widow, also helped out. Arno Bach emptied their chamber pot at night and informed the brothers of the situation on the front. The arrangement was particularly

JUREK ROZENEK, FRIEDA LÖSER, LUISE AND ALFRED GRIESMANN, MARGARETE AND ARNO BACH, MICHAEL ROZENEK (LEFT TO RIGHT) IN NIEDERSCHMIEDEBERG, JUNE 29, 1945

dangerous because Michael Rozenek had tuberculosis and his loud coughing could have given them away.

On May 8, the Rozeneks were liberated by the Soviet army. They had a difficult time convincing the commander that they had been concentration camp prisoners. On their suggestion, Arno Bach was appointed mayor by the Soviets. The Rozeneks lived in Berlin until 1951, when they emigrated to Buenos Aires, where a sister of theirs was living. Miguel Rozenek, as he was then called, visited his helpers in Niederschmiedeberg in 1987 and 1989 and initiated their being honored by the Israeli Holocaust memorial Yad Vashem.

BIBLIOGRAPHY Rozenek, Michael. *"Wie wird es einmal enden?" Bericht des ehemaligen jüdischen Häftlings Michael Rozenek über seine Rettung*, edited by Gedenkstätte Buchenwald. Weimar: Gutenberg Buchdruckerei, 1991.

MICHAEL (LEFT; 1914–1990) AND JUREK (RIGHT; 1918–1995) ROZENEK WITH ARNO BACH (1904–2007); THE ROZENEKS PUT THEIR CAMP CLOTHING BACK ON FOR THIS PHOTO, TAKEN ON JUNE 29, 1945, IN FRONT OF THE SHED IN WHICH THEY HID.

Odyssey through Germany

Jewish journalist Wilhelm Meyer was an editor for the Ullstein publishing house until 1933. When he died in the fall of 1942, friends urged his widow Susanne to go into hiding. Their thirteen-year-old son had been able to escape to England in 1939. The newspaper illustrator and Social Democrat Alois Florath, in particular, urged Susanne Meyer to flee. He had heard from a policeman that Jews in Poland were being murdered with carbon-monoxide gas.

Friedrich Kroner, former Ullstein editor-in-chief, introduced Susanne Meyer to Eduard Stadtler, a former politician in the right-wing German National People's Party, who played an ignominious role at Ullstein after 1933. In 1943 he became a helper, saving Meyer's life. Through his contacts to conservative opponents of the Nazi regime, Stadtler arranged her first illegal lodgings with an acquaintance.

On the morning of January 7, 1943, Susanne Meyer left her apartment without her Yellow Star and boarded a train to Küstrin. This step marked the beginning of a dramatic odyssey crisscrossing Germany. Meyer's first stop was in the area around Landsberg an der Warthe (Polish: Gorzów Wielkopolski). She was picked up at the Lipke train station by manor owner Hans-Wolfgang Lent and his wife Ingeborg. The couple, parents of two sons, didn't know the Jewish woman from Berlin, but had agreed to take her in. When six weeks later someone in the circle of the manor owner was arrested, Meyer fled to Berlin, where Stadtler helped her again. He referred her to lodgings with several Catholic families in Düsseldorf who were relatives of his wife.

When Susanne Meyer again returned to Berlin in the summer of 1943, Alois Florath helped her find lodgings in Kagar, a village near Rheinsberg in Brandenburg. Starting in 1943, Kagar was a refuge also for non-Jewish opponents of the Nazi regime. Georg Steffen, a farmer and, like his Huguenot ancestors, village mayor of Kagar, and his wife Elise offered refuge during the war to people suffering racist and political persecution. Among those who found temporary shelter in their guesthouse and pension were Otto Suhr, later mayor of Berlin, and his Jewish wife Susanne. Susanne Meyer was taken in on numerous occasions. She also hid temporarily in the summerhouse of her former neighbor in Berlin, Arthur Veit, at Mellensee, and she stayed for a few months with Dr. Mathilde Stoltenhoff, a physician in

ALOIS FLORATH (1897–1944), CA. 1943

Berlin-Lichterfelde. Meyer helped her in the household and in her practice.

Berlin journalist Herta Zerna was a member of the Social Democratic Party until 1933. Toward the end of the war she let Susanne Meyer stay with her and her mother in their small house in Kagar, which is where Meyer was when the war ended. A short time later she returned to Berlin, where after six years she finally saw her son again, who had since become a British soldier. She married her helper Arthur Veit. Georg Steffen was denounced in July 1945 and subsequently interned in the Soviet special camp in Jamlitz near Lieberose. He died there in June 1946 at the age of fifty-five.

BIBLIOGRAPHY Kosmala, Beate. "Zuflucht für Verfolgte: Kagar bei Rheinsberg." In *Juden in Rheinsberg: Eine Spurensuche*, edited by Peter Böthig and Stefanie Oswald, 163–170. Neuruppin, Germany: Edition Rieger, 2005. | Kosmala, Beate. "Solidarität mit verfolgten Kollegen: Die Rettung von Susanne Meyer." In *Im Namen der Eule*, edited by Christoph Hamann, Konstanze Lindemann et al., 94–100. 2nd rev. ed. Berlin: Trafo, forthcoming.

SUSANNE MEYER (1902–1987) WITH HER SON HANS ULRICH (B. 1926), WHO HAD SINCE BECOME A BRITISH SOLDIER, LATE 1945 IN BERLIN

Struggling Underground from Day to Day

Ilse Basch was forced to leave secondary school in 1935; she graduated from a commercial school and worked as a secretary. After 1933, interior designer Werner Rewald was allowed to work only as an upholsterer because he was Jewish. Basch and Rewald were married in 1938 in Berlin. Their plans to emigrate failed when the war started in 1939. Beginning in the fall of 1939, Werner had to do harvesting work and later forced labor for the German state railroad. Fritz Wolzenburg, his foreman, retained him, thus saving him from deportation. Ilse Rewald had to do forced labor in an armaments factory. Throughout 1942 the Rewalds continued to learn more about the camps "in the East," the destination of the deportations. Their friends Paul and Elli Fromm, who had heard about Jews who went underground to avoid the imminent deportations, offered Werner Rewald a place to hide. After a long search, Ilse Rewald found lodgings with Käthe Pickardt, the Christian widow of a Jewish doctor, and her daughter Ursula.

On January 11, 1943, the Rewalds went into hiding in their prearranged lodgings and kept in contact with each other as best they could. As of late February 1943, spouses in mixed marriages were also threatened with deportation, so Werner Rewald no longer could stay with the Fromms. As an apartment manager, however, Paul Fromm was able to refer him to other places to stay, though Werner Rewald couldn't stay anywhere for very long. Sometimes he rented a room in a pension, sometimes he spent the night in a summerhouse. During the day he did all kinds of jobs in exchange for food or nightly lodgings. Ilse Rewald worked as domestic help or did secretarial work. Ilse and Werner Rewald worried about each other with every air raid.

Elisabeth Litt, a teacher, had good relations with the Jewish Basch family going back to Ilse's elementary school days. She heard about the Rewalds' harried lives in hiding. Though suffering from tuberculosis, she helped them by regularly writing letters to an agreed-upon address, sending food, and giving them courage to endure. Elisabeth Litt died in 1944 in a sanatorium for tuberculosis.

Ilse Rewald's motherly friend Elsa Chotzen and her oldest son Joseph ("Eppi") could not give the Rewalds lodging because they were at risk themselves, but they took the Rewalds' important documents and photographs for safekeeping. During the

Marriage of Ilse (1918–2005) and Werner (1907–1992) Rewald, Berlin, December 20, 1938 day the harried couple was welcome to visit anytime and relax for a few hours.

German railroad inspector Fritz Wolzenburg obtained authentic German railroad ID cards for the Rewalds. Werner Rewald, in particular, felt safer with the documents, as men of military age often had their papers checked.

From November 1943 on, Werner Rewald also stayed with the Pickardts, but when the apartment was destroyed in an air raid in late January 1944, they had to find new lodgings. Through someone Ilse Rewald had met while doing forced labor, she heard about the musicians Cornelia and Hanning Schröder. Although they had a mixed marriage they still ventured to take the Rewalds into their home in Berlin-Zehlendorf. After Cornelia Schröder and her ten-year-old daughter Nele moved to Mecklenburg because of the air raids, a Wehrmacht officer was quartered in their home. The Rewalds assumed a made-up, yet believable identity in his presence. Ilse and Werner Rewald survived the war at Hanning Schröder's, who summarized the motives for his actions by saying, "I wanted to counter the horrors of the concentration camps with my concentrated effort."

BIBLIOGRAPHY Eckhardt, Ulrich, and Andreas Nachama, eds. *Jüdische Berliner: Leben nach der Schoa; 14 Gespräche.* Berlin: Jaron, 2003. See esp. 189–207. | Köhler, Jochen. *Klettern in der Großstadt: Geschichten vom Überleben in Berlin zwischen 1933 und 1945.* Berlin: Wagenbach, 1981. | Rewald, Ilse. *Berliner, die uns halfen, die Hitlerdiktatur zu überleben.* Beiträge zum Widerstand 1933–1945, vol. 6. Berlin: Gedenkstätte Deutscher Widerstand, 1985. | Schieb, Barbara. *Nachricht von Chotzen: "Wer immer hofft, stirbt singend."* Berlin: Hentrich, 2000.

CORNELIA (RIGHT) AND HANNING SCHRÖDER WITH DAUGHTER NELE, IN DARGUN, MECKLENBURG, 1948

Hidden in the Bread Car

When Edith Felix, a young Czech Jew, returned from doing forced labor to her room in Berlin-Friedrichshain, she learned that her Jewish landlady had been picked up by the Gestapo. Fearing that she too would be deported, Felix fled. In Berlin-Karow she asked Ruth Schneider, the sister of a friend and a staunch opponent of the regime, for help.

Felix thus became involved with a circle of helpers who were active in the communist resistance. Ruth Schneider lived in the house of her coworker, Käthe Schulz. Both were part of a left-wing resistance cell of employees at the C. Müller rubber works. They already had experience in finding illegal quarters, as a large number of labor movement functionaries went underground as of 1933 and were in need of places to hide. Schulz and Schneider took in Edith Felix and also asked relatives for assistance.

Felix was able to alternate hiding with the two women and with the family of Käthe Schulz's sister Hertha Hellige in Berlin-Frohnau. In this house, Hertha and Heinrich Hellige, Martha and Walter Hellige, and a total of five children lived together under one roof. As members of the Communist Party, which was banned in 1933, the Helliges belonged to an underground resistance cell.

Walter Hellige had already been convicted of political resistance in 1935 and sentenced to fifteen months' imprisonment. No longer allowed to work as a banker, he delivered bread until the end of the war. His delivery vehicle provided a great service for their resistance activities. He could use it inconspicuously for courier trips to transport subversive materials and people, and this is how Edith Felix was able to change quarters safely. Her last lodgings before the war ended were at the home of Else Seibler —a relative of Ruth Schneider—and her partner Bernhard Reiß in Berlin-Moabit.

Edith Felix was not the only one hidden within this circle of helpers. Hellige's friends and political comrades Gertrud and Karl Neuhof hid a communist official in the neighborhood. When he was discovered, the Gestapo also arrested his helpers. Karl Neuhof, who was of Jewish descent, was shot, and his Gentile wife was sent to prison for almost a year.

In 1944, Edith Felix's helpers made contact with the communist resistance organization around Anton Saefkow and Franz Jacob, which aimed to link resistance groups scattered throughout the city. Käthe Schulz and Ruth Schneider made their home

WALTER HELLIGE'S BREAD DELIVERY CAR IN 1940, WITH HERTHA HELLIGE STANDING AT THE FRONT OF THE CAR AND MARTHA HELLIGE AT THE BACK;

A NEIGHBOR IS SITTING IN THE CAR WITH TWO-YEAR-OLD INGRID HELLIGE

available for secret meetings of the Saefkow-Jacob organization. There they met Gerhard Danelius, a young communist from a Jewish family. He had gone into hiding in 1942 and often was able to stay with the two women. When they had to move with their company to Vogtland, they left him their house, where together with his girlfriend he had a safe hiding place until the end of the war.

Edith Felix left her hiding place in Seibler and Reiß's courtyard apartment in Berlin-Moabit in April 1945. She made her way to Prague to find out what happened to her family. She survived.

BIBLIOGRAPHY Hochmuth, Ursel. *Illegale KPD und Bewegung "Freies Deutschland" in Berlin und Brandenburg 1942–1945: Biographien und Zeugnisse aus der Widerstandsorganisation um Saefkow, Jacob und Bästlein*. Journals of the German Resistance Memorial Center, series A, vol. 4. Berlin: Gedenkstätte Deutscher Widerstand, 1998. | Lammel, Inge, ed. *Jüdisches Leben in Pankow: Eine zeitgeschichtliche Dokumentation*, edited by Bund der Antifaschisten Berlin-Pankow. Berlin: Edition Hentrich, 1993. See esp. 170–172. | Neuhof, Peter. *Als die Braunen kamen: Eine Berliner jüdische Familie im Widerstand*. Bonn: Pahl-Rugenstein, 2006.

EDITH FELIX (1916–1982), SHORTLY BEFORE SHE WENT INTO HIDING, CA. 1940

Eva and Carl Hermann

Eva Hermann and her husband Carl Hermann, a physicist, were committed pacifists and opponents of the Nazi regime. Around 1934 they joined the religious community of the Quakers in Mannheim. Especially Eva Hermann, who was not gainfully employed since their marriage in 1924, put all her energy into supporting Jews. Thanks to her contacts, including those to the Quakers in England, she was able to help Jews enter Great Britain despite the strict immigration requirements there. During the November Pogrom of 1938, the Hermanns took in a Jewish acquaintance, thereby protecting him from being sent to a concentration camp. When in 1940 the Jews of Mannheim were already being deported to southern France, the Hermanns sent food packages and encouraging letters to the Gurs camp. They faced their greatest challenge in early 1943: when Eva Hermann's former Jewish classmate Hilde Rosenthal and her husband Fritz evaded deportation from Berlin, they asked the Hermanns for assistance. The Quaker couple hid the Rosenthals in their apartment for four weeks—despite the risk this presented especially for their two young children.

In April 1943, after the arrest of Gertrud Luckner—another person who helped the Rosenthals—the Gestapo located the Jewish couple while they were staying with an acquaintance in Saarbrücken. Fritz Rosenthal committed suicide when he was arrested. His wife Hilde was deported to the Theresienstadt ghetto and from there, in October 1944, to the Auschwitz-Birkenau extermination camp, where she was murdered.

Eva and Carl Hermann were arrested in Mannheim in the spring of 1943. During their interrogation, they both admitted to having hidden the Rosenthals out of compassion and to having listened to foreign radio broadcasts with them, even though this was strictly forbidden since the start of the war. The couple was charged with so-called radio broadcast crimes in July 1943. Whereas the Gestapo decree against helping Jews was enforced arbitrarily, the law regarding radio crimes was unambiguous: in particularly severe cases, the death penalty could be imposed. For listening to British radio and spreading the news they heard, Carl Hermann was sentenced to eight years of penal servitude; Eva Hermann received a three-year sentence. The fact that Carl Hermann's research for the IG Farben chemical company in Ludwigshafen was deemed vital to the war effort might have led to their not receiving the maximum sentence. Carl Hermann had

1 EVA HERMANN (1900–1997), 1936   2 CARL HERMANN (1898–1961), CA. 1939

to continue his research during his imprisonment. He and his wife both survived various penal institutions.

After the war, Carl Hermann was a professor of crystallography in Marburg until his death in 1961. Eva Hermann was active in encouraging Christian-Jewish dialogue. The couple was honored several times in Israel and the Federal Republic of Germany for their courageous efforts.

BIBLIOGRAPHY Borgstedt, Angela. "Eva und Dr. Carl Hermann: Zwei Mannheimer Quäker und ihre Hilfe für Verfolgte des NS-Regimes." *Badische Heimat* 79 (1999): 183–189. | Fliedner, Hans-Joachim. *Die Judenverfolgung in Mannheim 1933–1945.* Vol. 2. Stuttgart: W. Kohlhammer, 1971. See esp. 95–101, 380–384.

HILDE ROSENTHAL (1896–1944), AFTER 1936

Agnes Wendland

Agnes Crolow and the theologian Walter Wendland married in 1912. Their children Ruth, Angelika, and Arndt were born in 1913, 1915, and 1919, respectively. In 1916, Walter Wendland became pastor of the Gethsemane parish in the district of Prenzlauer Berg in Berlin. His wife not only raised their children, but also, as the pastor's wife, organized the Women's Charity in the congregation. Anyone who rang the bell of the parsonage received a warm welcome. The large circle of friends and acquaintances of the family of five was comprised of Christians and Jews—no distinctions were made. Ruth began studying theology in 1933 in Berlin and Basel; Angelika started business school in 1935. All of the Wendland family members joined the Protestant Confessing Church in 1934. After completing secondary school, Arndt was drafted into the Wehrmacht and killed in action in 1942.

Agnes Wendland's knowledge of the life-threatening situation facing Jews motivated her to act: starting in 1943, she offered lodgings in the parsonage to Jews who went underground. In the summer of 1943 she took in Rita Neumann, a Jew in hiding; a few weeks later, Rita's seventeen-year-old brother Ralph was allowed to stay there as well. Agnes Wendland did not reveal the siblings' true identity to her husband, in order not to burden him as pastor. The Neumanns got to know other helpers in the Wendlands' circle of friends, who arranged jobs, documents, and additional means of support for them. The older daughter, Ruth Wendland, became a vicar at a church in Berlin-Zehlendorf in October 1943. Her sister Angelika married Günther Rutenborn, who as of September 1943 served as minister in the Brandenburg town of Senzke. The Neumann siblings were also warmly welcomed there. Georg Remak, a lawyer who had gone into hiding, was given refuge in the parsonage by Agnes Wendland in the fall of 1944. After fleeing from a camp in France, Wolfgang Hammerschmidt went to Berlin and was taken in by the Wendland family for the Christmas holidays in 1944.

When Ralph Neumann was discovered in February 1945, it led to Agnes Wendland's arrest as well. Due to her poor state of health, she was released after three weeks in custody, but her daughter Ruth had to spend another three weeks in Gestapo custody in her place. When Rita, too, was arrested, the siblings were reunited as prisoners in the Jewish Hospital on Iranische Strasse, where the Gestapo had set up a pre-deportation assem-

AGNES (1891–1946) AND WALTER WENDLAND IN THE ENVIRONS OF BERLIN, 1935

bly camp. They managed to escape from there during an air raid in late March 1945. They made their way to prison chaplain Harald Poelchau, who referred them in April to journalist Ruth Andreas-Friedrich, an active opponent of the regime. Together with Ruth Wendland, Ralph Neumann participated in the "Nein" ("No") action organized by the "Uncle Emil" resistance group on the night of April 18, 1945. The large white "Nein" painted on building facades in many districts of Berlin were courageous signs of opposition to the war.

After the war, Agnes Wendland became seriously ill. Ralph and Rita Neumann emigrated to the United States in 1946, where they learned of the death of their helper in August 1946, at the age of just 55 years.

Agnes Wendland and her daughter Ruth Wendland were honored in 1975 by the Israeli Holocaust memorial Yad Vashem as Righteous Among the Nations.

BIBLIOGRAPHY Grossmann, Kurt R. *Die unbesungenen Helden: Menschen in Deutschlands dunklen Tagen*. Frankfurt: Ullstein, 1984. See esp. 68–72. | Neuman, Ralph. *Memories from My Early Life in Germany 1926–1946*. Berlin: Gedenkstätte Deutscher Widerstand, 2006. | Sandvoß, Hans-Rainer. "Bekennende Gemeinde Gethsemane." In *Widerstand in Prenzlauer Berg und Weißensee*, 270–71. Vol. 12 of *Widerstand in Berlin von 1933 bis 1945*. Berlin: Gedenkstätte Deutscher Widerstand, 2000. | See, Wolfgang, and Rudolf Weckerling. "Kirchenfrau im Abseits: Ruth Wendland." In *Frauen im Kirchenkampf: Beispiele aus der Bekennenden Kirche Berlin-Brandenburg*, 53–59. Berlin: Wichern, 1984.

1 RITA NEUMANN (1919–1977), BERLIN, 1946   2 RALPH NEUMANN (B. 1926), BERLIN, 1946

Eugen Herman-Friede

Eugen Herman was born in 1926 in Berlin to a Russian-Jewish couple. After his parents separated a short time later, he grew up with his mother Anja and his Gentile stepfather Julius Friede. Eugen attended the Jewish Middle School starting in 1936. When he was fifteen, he began to show an interest in photography. He used his stepfather's camera because Jews were prohibited from owning one. Thus, there exist some rare photographs from 1942 of his school class, as well as photographs taken at Eugen's forced labor job at the Jewish Cemetery in Weissensee. When Eugen had to go into hiding in late January 1943, Julius Friede brought him to the first illegal quarters that had been arranged: Eugen was able to stay for two weeks with Julius Friede's gas station attendant. He then was taken in by the Horn family, who were regime opponents, in Berlin-Blankenburg. To keep himself occupied, Eugen had the camera with him in hiding. He photographed his helpers, had them take pictures of him, developed his film himself, and put together a photo album that is on display in the Silent Heroes Memorial Center.

In August 1943, Eugen was referred to the family of a court clerk, Hans Winkler, in Luckenwalde, where he took part in the founding of the resistance group Gemeinschaft für Frieden und Aufbau (Community for Peace and Reconstruction). Hans Winkler and Werner Scharff, a Jew who had escaped from the Theresienstadt ghetto, planned leaflet actions calling for resistance to the war. Eugen Herman-Friede participated enthusiastically in all the group's activities. Werner Scharff mobilized his friends in Berlin, and Hans Winkler motivated some trustworthy acquaintances in Luckenwalde to take action. Eugen met all of them: the butcher, the cafeteria proprietor, the restaurant owner, the small industrialist, and the waiter who was drafted into the Wehrmacht. They all helped out with forged documents, food, and lodgings. Ten Jewish women and men who were living illegally in Berlin were given refuge in Luckenwalde. They also participated in making and circulating two leaflets in April and August 1944.

Hans Winkler, Werner Scharff, and others in the group were arrested by the Gestapo in October 1944, while Eugen and his parents were living illegally in a guesthouse in Luckenwalde. He took his last photographs on the roof there in the fall of 1944. The Gestapo tracked down the Friede family in December 1944.

EUGEN HERMAN-FRIEDE'S SEVENTEENTH BIRTHDAY, CELEBRATED IN HIDING; FROM LEFT: JULIUS FRIEDE, ANJA FRIEDE, UNKNOWN, GERTRUD HORN, EUGEN HERMAN-FRIEDE, EWALD HORN, WILLI BREMEYER, GRETE RADO, IN BERLIN-BLANKENBURG, APRIL 23, 1943

Julius Friede committed suicide in the police prison in Berlin; Eugen's mother Anja was deported to the Theresienstadt ghetto in early February 1945. Unexpectedly released from a Berlin prison, Eugen Herman-Friede experienced the end of the war in early May 1945 in the center of Berlin. Anja Friede returned to Berlin from Theresienstadt in June 1945.

Frida and Hans Winkler were honored posthumously in 2008 by the Israeli Holocaust memorial Yad Vashem as Righteous Among the Nations.

BIBLIOGRAPHY Herman-Friede, Eugen. *Für Freudensprünge keine Zeit: Erinnerungen an Illegalität und Aufbegehren 1942–1948*, with an afterword by Barbara Schieb-Samizadeh. Berlin: Metropol, 1991. | Herman-Friede, Eugen. *Abgetaucht! Als U-Boot im Widerstand*. Hildesheim, Germany: Gerstenberg, 2004. | Schieb-Samizadeh, Barbara. "Die Gemeinschaft für Frieden und Aufbau." In *Juden im Widerstand: Drei Gruppen zwischen Überlebenskampf und politischer Aktion, Berlin 1939–1945*, edited by Wilfried Löhken and Werner Vathke, 37–81. Berlin: Hentrich, 1993.

[1] HANS WINKLER (1906–1987), LUCKENWALDE, 1943   [2] WERNER SCHARFF (1912–1945), BERLIN, CA. 1941

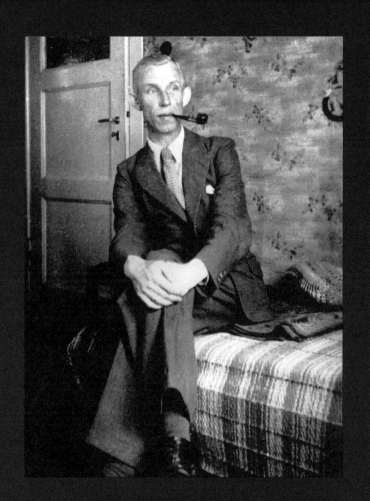

Alice Löwenthal

In 1942 the Jewish seamstress Alice Löwenthal was living with her husband Adolf and her young daughters Ruth and Brigitte in a so-called Jewish apartment in the district of Prenzlauer Berg in Berlin. They shared the space with their aunt Martha Sussmann, the former owner of the apartment building. In these oppressive times, Löwenthal's children lived with a feeling of relative security until their 63-year-old great-aunt Martha was deported to the Theresienstadt ghetto on September 4, 1942.

When Adolf Löwenthal was arrested on February 27, 1943, during the so-called Factory Action, their non-Jewish neighbor Johannes Gabriel appealed to Alice to go into hiding with her daughters. He helped them with their preparations, and they barely escaped deportation. Alice Löwenthal later reported, "I got my two girls dressed at five in the morning and left the apartment at the crack of dawn. As I later heard from other residents, I got out in the nick of time, because the Gestapo van drove up at six to 'pick us up.'"

They had to change quarters several times. A friend referred her to a place to stay in Strausberg, east of Berlin, with Luise Nickel, who was living in her weekend house in Brandenburg because of the air raids on Berlin. The 59-year-old widow, a feisty woman and a communist, earned her livelihood as an ironer. When the situation there became too risky, mother and daughters again had to "disappear."

The desperate woman ventured to take a train ride with the girls to Weimar in May 1943. When the acquaintance with whom they were supposed to stay pretended that she wasn't at home, Walter Schmidt, a former policeman, spontaneously offered to help. His cousin Elly Möller, a housewife with no children of her own, took in the two girls. She knew the sisters were Jewish, but nevertheless sometimes passed them on to other families in Weimar and Apolda.

Believing her children were safe, Alice Löwenthal was relieved and returned to Berlin. Every month she sent food that she had purchased on the black market to Weimar. She found lodgings with various helpers and worked as a sewer. Often she was taken in by Alfred Viere, who had a haulage company. As a supporter of the illegal Communist Party, he had been incarcerated after 1933 in the Lichtenburg concentration camp near Torgau. In their pet shop, which had been closed, he and his wife Martha

1 Alice Löwenthal's daughters Ruth (1937–1944) and Brigitte Süssmann (1939–1944), at Scharmützelsee, a lake in Brandenburg, 1941

2 Alice Löwenthal (1909–1987), 1945

hid not only Alice Löwenthal but also Rolf Themal. In late 1943, Löwenthal moved back in with Luise Nickel in Strausberg, who also harbored others escaping persecution.

Just as she had always hoped, in late April 1945 Alice Löwenthal opened the door to her undestroyed apartment, using her own key, which she had always kept with her. Not until several months later did she hear about the fate of her daughters, from whom she had received no news since early 1944. Ruth and Brigitte were denounced in June 1944, and the Gestapo had them "taken away" from Weimar. They were deported from Berlin to the Auschwitz-Birkenau extermination camp in August 1944, where they were murdered.

Alice Löwenthal had lost her husband, her children, and all her relatives. She remained in Berlin-Prenzlauer Berg and married Willy Nickel, the son of her helper Luise. Their daughter Eva was born in 1948.

BIBLIOGRAPHY Kosmala, Beate. "Das kurze Leben von Ruth und Gittel Süssmann." In *Gegen das Vergessen: Erinnerungen an das Jüdische Kinderheim Fehrbelliner Straße 92 Berlin-Prenzlauer Berg*, edited by Inge Franken, 87–100. Berlin: text, 2005. | Scheer, Regina. "Evas Haus: Alice Löwenthal und ihre Töchter, Christinenstraße 35." In *Leben mit der Erinnerung: Jüdische Geschichte in Prenzlauer Berg*, edited by Kulturamt Prenzlauer Berg, 97–102. Berlin: Edition Hentrich, 1997.

LUISE NICKEL (1885–1968) WITH HER DAUGHTER-IN-LAW ALICE (LEFT), MARTHA VIERE (RIGHT), AND GRANDDAUGHTER EVA, 1951

Maria Gräfin von Maltzan

Maria Gräfin von Maltzan was born in 1909 on the Militsch estate near Breslau (now Wrocław). In 1933, at the age of 24, she completed her doctorate in the natural sciences in Munich. Maria von Maltzan moved to Berlin in 1936, where she started studying veterinary medicine in 1940. She and the Jewish writer Hans Hirschel became friends in 1939. He had been head of the sales department for a large company until he was dismissed in 1938. Although it was risky to have contact with Jews, she regularly visited him and his mother Lucie Hirschel in their apartment.

When Hans Hirschel's mother was deported in March 1942 and he was faced with the prospect of being deported himself, Maria von Maltzan offered to hide him in her small two-room apartment in the Wilmersdorf district of Berlin. They couldn't know at the time that he would end up spending three years there in hiding.

In mid-1943 the Gestapo suddenly appeared at the door to search the apartment, as neighbors had denounced Maria von Maltzan. Hirschel managed to get into his hiding space in a convertible sofa just in time. Thanks to his girlfriend, who sat on the couch and maintained her cool throughout the interrogation, keeping the Gestapo men from opening the couch, he was not discovered. Maria von Maltzan also sheltered other people temporarily, including Charlotte Bamberg, who had lost her previous lodgings and stayed with Maltzan for several weeks in her apartment at Detmolder Strasse 11.

In 1943, Maria von Maltzan completed her studies and became the director of an animal shelter. She also was assigned to work as a meat inspector at a slaughterhouse, which made it easier for her to feed those she had in hiding.

In August 1943, Maria von Maltzan was involved in "Operation Swedish Furniture," a rescue action carried out by Erik Perwe, pastor of the Swedish Victoria congregation in Berlin-Wilmersdorf. Together with the secretary of his congregation Erik Wesslén, Perwe helped Jews escape to Sweden. The courageous veterinarian led a group of Jews at night to an agreed location at the train tracks in Frohnau, in northern Berlin. A train carrying the furniture of Swedes returning home made a stop there. Swedish helpers opened the sealed doors and unloaded some of the cargo to make room for the refugees to board the

<u>1</u> Maria Gräfin von Maltzan (1909–1997), ca. 1942   <u>2</u> Hans Hirschel (1900–1974) in hiding, ca. 1943

train. Then the cars were resealed. After one such action, Maria von Maltzan escaped an SS patrol in the forest by a hair's breadth.

Toward the end of the war, she received a photo ID for Hans Hirschel as "Commissioner for the overall defense of Berlin" from Werner Keller, a division leader in the Reich Ministry for Armaments and War Production, who had also helped others in hiding. This document enabled Hirschel to leave his hiding place. In March 1945, Maria von Maltzan took in the seriously ill Wolfgang Hammerschmidt for a few days and provided him with neces-sary medical care. Hammerschmidt was deemed a so-called first-degree Mischling (of "mixed blood") and had escaped from the Organization Todt.

Hans Hirschel and Maria Gräfin von Maltzan were in Berlin when the war ended in late April 1945. They married the following year. Maria von Maltzan later opened a practice for veterinary medicine in Berlin-Kreuzberg. Maria Gräfin von Maltzan was honored in 1987 by the Israeli Holocaust memorial Yad Vashem as Righteous Among the Nations.

BIBLIOGRAPHY Maltzan, Maria Gräfin von. *Schlage die Trommel und fürchte Dich nicht: Erinnerungen.* Frankfurt: Ullstein, 1988. | Perwe, Johan. *Bombprästen: Erik Perwe på uppdrag i Berlin under andra världskriget* (The Bomb Pastor: Erik Perwe's Mission in Berlin during the Second World War). Stockholm: Carlsson, 2006.

PASTOR ERIK PERWE, CA. 1943

Oskar and Emilie Schindler

Oskar Schindler was born in 1908 in the Moravian city of Zwittau. He married Emilie Pelzl, one year his senior, in 1928. Around 1935 he joined the Nazi-oriented Sudeten German Party (SdP). He became a counterintelligence agent in the German Wehrmacht and joined the Nazi Party (NSDAP) in 1939. In late 1939, at the age of 31, Schindler, a businessman, moved to the German-occupied Polish city of Krakow and took over a formerly Jewish-owned enamel works there. By producing dishes for the Wehrmacht and trading on the black market, Schindler soon started making considerable profits. He lived like a lord and was considered a lady's man. He kept up good relations with administrative officials, members of the military, and SS personnel.

At first the young businessman hired Poles as inexpensive labor, but starting in 1941 he increasingly used Jewish forced laborers, as they were cheaper than Polish workers. Schindler was soon an eyewitness to the brutal deportations from the Krakow ghetto, which had a profound effect on him. He went through a transformation at that time and started working out ways to protect his Jewish workers.

After the bloody liquidation of the Krakow ghetto in March 1943, the remaining 8,000 prisoners were interned in the Płaszów concentration camp, near Krakow. Schindler gained the favor of the sadistic camp commander Amon Göth through ostentatious gifts and drinking sprees. With Göth's support, Schindler received authorization to set up a separate subcamp on his own factory grounds, which offered his workers a certain degree of protection.

In Płaszów, Schindler also got to know Göth's secretary, the Jewish prisoner Mietek Pemper, and gained his trust. Pemper urged Schindler to start producing shell parts as well, in order to maintain his company as a munitions factory. Schindler followed his advice.

When thousands of prisoners were again being deported from the Płaszów camp to Auschwitz in the summer of 1944, a dramatic race against time started for Schindler. The once profit-oriented businessman became a rescuer of human lives. In order to protect his forced workers, he engaged in arduous negotiations to move his artillery shell production site from Krakow to Brünnlitz in his native Moravia. He invested his entire personal assets into saving his workers.

EMILIE SCHINDLER (1907–2001) AND OSKAR SCHINDLER (1908–1974), CA. 1949

In October 1944 the first list of 1,000 Jews was drawn up: 700 men and 300 women whom he took with him to his factory in Brünnlitz, thereby saving them from further deportation and death marches. Among the names were those of Mietek Pemper and Izak Stern, a friend of Schindler from Płaszów, and their families. When the women were transported to Auschwitz-Birkenau instead of Brünnlitz, Schindler intervened persistently on their behalf until they were finally brought to Brünnlitz several weeks later.

Emilie Schindler worked untiringly to help feed the forced laborers in the factory in Brünnlitz, a subcamp of the Gross-Rosen concentration camp. In January 1945, Oskar Schindler took in another transport of prisoners who had almost frozen to death, and his wife cared for them, enabling more to survive. All told, Oskar and Emilie Schindler were able to save at least 1,100 people.

Oskar and Emilie Schindler were honored by the Israeli Holocaust memorial Yad Vashem as Righteous Among the Nations.

BIBLIOGRAPHY Crowe, David M. *Oskar Schindler: The Untold Account of His Life, Wartime Activities, and the True Story Behind the List*. Cambridge, MA: Westview Press, 2004. | Müller-Madej, Stella. *A Girl from Schindler's List*, translated by William R. Brand. London: Polish Cultural Foundation, 1997. | Pemper, Mieczysław (Mietek), with Viktoria Hertling, assisted by Marie Elisabeth Müller. *The Road to Rescue: the Untold Story of Schindler's List*, translated by David Dollenmayer. New York: Other Press, 2008. | Schindler, Emilie, with Erika Rosenberg. *Where Light and Shadow Meet: A Memoir*, translated by Dolores M. Koch. New York: W. W. Norton, 1997.

1 IZAK STERN (1901–1969), SPRING 1949

2 MIETEK PEMPER (B. 1920), IN SEPTEMBER 1946 AT THE KRAKOW TRIAL OF AMON GÖTH, COMMANDER OF THE PŁASZÓW CONCENTRATION CAMP

Heinrich and Marie List

Heinrich and Marie List lived on and ran a farm in Ernsbach, a small village in the Odenwald hills in the state of Hesse. They had two grown children. One day in mid-November 1941, Ferdinand Strauss, a 39-year-old Jewish businessman from the neighboring town of Michelstadt, was suddenly standing at the Lists' door. He was on the run from the immediate threat of deportation, after having already been interned in the Buchenwald concentration camp for a month following the November Pogrom in 1938. He came to ask the farmers for help, as they used to be good customers in his family's clothing store. Suddenly confronted with the desperate situation of the Jewish man, Marie List did not hesitate to take Strauss in, even though it was very risky in a village where everyone knew everyone else. Her husband also agreed when he returned home from working in the fields.

But Strauss's hiding place was exposed in March 1942: a Polish forced laborer who was working on List's farm told another farmer about the presence of a suspicious stranger. This farmer grew distrustful and filed a report with the mayor, who then informed the police. Heinrich and Marie List were interrogated, and they ultimately admitted to having hidden Ferdinand Strauss. In answer to the officer's question as to why he took in the Jew, the 60-year-old farmer answered, "because we knew each other very well and used to have good business relations, so I was struck with compassion and decided to shelter him." The Gestapo arrested Heinrich List in April 1942. Marie List received only a severe warning, even though she had been just as involved as her husband in helping Strauss. In view of the serious food shortage, the Gestapo probably did not want the farm to be left untended. After three months in the Gestapo prison in Darmstadt, Heinrich List was deported to the Dachau concentration camp. He died there on October 5, 1942, as a result of the inhumane conditions of detention. Marie List also had to cope with the loss of their son, who fell as a soldier in 1944.

After the war the people of Ernsbach did not talk about the events on the List's farm and the betrayal by village residents. Long after Marie List's death in 1965, she and her husband were honored posthumously by the Israeli Holocaust memorial Yad Vashem in 1993. Heinrich List is among the Righteous Among the Nations from Germany who paid for their deeds with their lives.

HEINRICH (1882–1942) AND MARIE (1881–1965) LIST, 1930S

Ferdinand Strauss was able to escape to Switzerland in May 1942. He emigrated to the United States in 1946, where he built up a new livelihood as an accountant. He died in New York in 1983.

BIBLIOGRAPHY Schoppmann, Claudia. "'Da packte mich das Mitleid und ich beherbergte ihn.' Tödliche Folgen für einen Bauern im Odenwald." In *Sie blieben unsichtbar: Zeugnisse aus den Jahren 1941 bis 1945*, edited by Beate Kosmala and Claudia Schoppmann, 50–57. Berlin: Förderverein Blindes Vertrauen, 2006.

FERDINAND STRAUSS (1902–1983), 1930S

Cioma Schönhaus

Samson Schönhaus, called Cioma, was born in 1922 in Berlin. He was the only son in a family of Russian-Jewish immigrants. The family owned a mineral water company on Sophienstrasse in Berlin-Mitte, which was confiscated by the Nazis in 1938. Cioma Schönhaus had to leave his Gymnasium (secondary school) in 1937 and transfer to the Jewish Middle School. His training as a graphic artist was interrupted when he was conscripted to do construction work. As of 1942 he had to do forced labor in uniform and weapons production.

His parents Fanja and Boris Schönhaus were deported to German-occupied Poland in June 1942 and murdered there. The same fate was suffered by his grandmother and other relatives. Cioma Schönhaus was allowed to remain in Berlin because he worked in the armaments industry. He decided to resist. In preparation to go underground, he sold his parents' household effects before they could be confiscated so that he would have money to support himself. He evaded regulations wherever he could and met with opponents of the regime.

Schönhaus started forging documents for a group of Protestant Christians from the Confessing Church in Berlin-Dahlem who helped people in hiding. The talented young man developed his own method of switching the photographs and copying the official stamps to make them look very authentic. He soon started receiving new requests. In late September 1942 he stopped working in the factory and went underground. Through a room referral agency he sought lodging as a subletter from various landladies, to whom he introduced himself under a false name. A store at Waldstrasse 54 in Berlin-Moabit, which intermediaries had rented for him, served as his forgery workshop. He shared the space with Ludwig Lichtwitz, who was also in hiding. There he forged identity papers regularly brought to him by Franz Kaufmann, a Christian of Jewish descent. Schönhaus obtained a Russian passport for himself under the name Peter Petrov. When he lost it he was in greater danger than before and also lost his ostensible freedom to move around in Berlin.

Helene Jacobs, who was working together with Kaufmann, hid Schönhaus in her apartment, but in August 1943 the Gestapo tracked down his helpers. Franz Kaufmann, Helene Jacobs, and many others were arrested. Schönhaus decided to flee from Germany. With forged ID papers, he set off by bicycle in the direction

CIOMA SCHÖNHAUS (B. 1922), CA. 1940

of Lake Constance. In early October, near the village of Oehningen, he managed to cross the border unnoticed into the Swiss town of Stein am Rhein. Franz Kaufmann was shot while in Gestapo custody. Helene Jacobs was sentenced to two and a half years of penal servitude and remained in prison until the war ended.

In Switzerland, Schönhaus was finally able to complete his vocational training and then studied psychology and German language and literature. In 1953 he started his own graphic arts business. Helene Jacobs and he remained friends throughout their lives.

BIBLIOGRAPHY Jacobs, Helene. "Für die anderen da sein." In *Frauen leisten Widerstand 1933–1945: Lebensgeschichten nach Interviews und Dokumenten*, edited by Gerda Szepansky, 57–90. Frankfurt: Fischer, 1985. | Rudolph, Katrin. *Hilfe beim Sprung ins Nichts: Franz Kaufmann und die Rettung von Juden und "nichtarischen" Christen*. Berlin: Metropol, 2005. | Schönhaus, Cioma. *The Forger: An Extraordinary Story of Survival in Wartime Berlin*. Edited and with an afterword by Marion Neiss. Translated by Alan Bance. Cambridge, MA: Da Capo Press, 2008.

HELENE JACOBS (1906–1993), 1936

Lilli Michalski

Lilli Brann was born in 1910 in Breslau into a Jewish business-man's family. In December 1933 she married Herbert Michalski, a Catholic businessman one year her senior. She converted to Catholicism shortly before the marriage. Herbert Michalski started a business as a traveling sales representative for pharmaceutical and cosmetic products in Görlitz. Having trained as an office clerk, Lilli Michalski handled the correspondence, bookkeeping, and other office work.

When their son Franz was born in 1934, the family hired sixteen-year-old Erna Scharf as a maid and nanny. Her father opposed the Nazi regime and had been arrested in 1933. He specifically chose the Michalski family to be certain that his daughter did not work for Nazis.

Herbert Michalski lost his business in 1938 because he refused to divorce Lilli. Although she had converted to Catholicism, she was still regarded as a Jew according to the Nuremberg race laws. Herbert Michalski was then hired by the Schwarzkopf company for its Berlin headquarters; he moved there in 1939. At Schwarzkopf he met Gerda Mez, a coworker with whom he could share his concerns. Also in 1939, Lilli Michalski moved with five-

year-old Franz to Breslau, where their second son Peter was born in 1940. Both children were baptized Catholic. In 1940 Herbert Michalski was drafted into the Wehrmacht; in 1942 he was given a dishonorable discharge because of his Jewish wife. Starting in October 1941, various members of Lilli's family were deported and killed.

Lilli and Herbert Michalski did not know how the Nazi regime planned to persecute Christians married to Jews and decided to go underground if necessary. When he was supposed to report for forced labor in October 1944, Herbert Michalski refused, and his wife fled their Breslau apartment with the children. Gerda Mez accompanied Lilli Michalski and the children on their escape from Breslau to Vienna and saved them by presenting her Aryan passport during ID controls on the train.

While Lilli and Herbert sought lodgings in the partisan region of Slovenia, they left the children in safety with their former nanny Erna Scharf's family in Thiemendorf near Görlitz. After wandering around for weeks, in February 1945 Lilli and Herbert Michalski accepted Gerda Mez's offer to stay with her in Tetschen-Bodenbach in the Sudeten mountains. She had been transferred

LILLI MICHALSKI (1910–1966) WITH HER SON FRANZ AND ERNA SCHARF (RIGHT) ON AN OUTING IN 1939

there by the Berlin Schwarzkopf headquarters for war-related reasons. Herbert and Lilli Michalski brought their two sons there as well in mid-February 1945, as the home of the Scharf family often was searched for deserters. Gerda Mez now shared her hotel room with the family of four. The hotel owner knew that Gerda Mez was hiding them, but did not denounce them. After weeks of trepidation waiting for liberation, constantly worrying about getting food, and struggling with Lilli's depression, the Michalski family lived to see the end of the war on May 8, 1945, in the neighboring town of Herrnskretschen.

PASSPORT OF GERDA MEZ (1911–2002), WHICH LILLI MICHALSKI PRESENTED FOR ID CHECKS ON THE TRAIN

Ehefrau

Lichtbild

Unterschrift des Paßinhabers

Gretel Metz

und seiner Ehefrau

Es wird hiermit bescheinigt, daß der Inhaber die durch das obenstehende Lichtbild dargestellte Person ist und die darunter befindliche Unterschrift eigenhändig vollzogen hat.

Berlin-Wilmersdorf den *4 April 1939*

2

PERSONENBESCHREIBUNG

Ehefrau

Beruf *Haarpflegespezialistin*

Geburtsort *Offenbach a/M.*

Geburtstag *2.9.11.*

Wohnort **Berlin-Wilmersdorf**

Gestalt *groß*

Gesicht *oval*

Farbe der Augen *blau*

Farbe des Haares *blond*

Besond. Kennzeichen *keine*

KINDER

Name	Alter	Geschlecht

3

The Development of the Silent Heroes Memorial Center

In recent years there has been growing public interest in the life stories of people who helped Jews suffering persecution during the Nazi dictatorship. Inspired by the association Gegen Vergessen—Für Demokratie (Against Oblivion—For Democracy), the comprehensive research project "Rescuing Jews in Nazi Germany 1933–1945" was conducted between 1997 and 2002 under the direction of Professor Wolfgang Benz at the Technical University of Berlin's Center for Research on Antisemitism. Films such as *Schindler's List* and numerous publications have also heightened interest in this subject.

Contemporary witness and journalist Inge Deutschkron was instrumental in the process of developing a student project at Berlin's University of Applied Sciences (FHTW) and later the "Blindes Vertrauen" (Blind Trust) exhibition into the Museum Otto Weidt's Workshop for the Blind at Rosenthaler Strasse 39 in the Mitte district of Berlin. During the Nazi era, mainly blind and deaf Jews were employed in this workshop under the protection of the brush manufacturer Otto Weidt (1883–1947). In 1999, following an initiative by the German government's Commissioner for Cultural and Media Affairs, Michael Naumann, the govern-

ment assumed responsibility for the museum. From that time on there were considerable efforts—such as from then German president Johannes Rau—to achieve further commemoration in Berlin of the helpers and people in hiding in Nazi Germany. In 2004 the building at Rosenthaler Straße 39 was purchased with funds from the German government and the Berlin Class Lottery Foundation which had been earmarked not only for the expansion of the Museum Otto Weidt's Workshop for the Blind but also for the establishment of a central Silent Heroes Memorial Center.

In April 2005 the German Resistance Memorial Center was commissioned with the conceptual and organizational planning of this new museum. In 2006 the permanent exhibition in the Museum Otto Weidt's Workshop for the Blind was first revised and expanded. The Silent Heroes Memorial Center was then realized in 2008. On the basis of research findings of the Center for Research on Antisemitism, a permanent exhibition was created that tells the story of people who helped Jews during the Nazi era. It depicts the desperate situation of Jews facing the threat of deportation, as well as the actions and motivations of the women and men who helped them. The example set by the helpers often described as "silent heroes" confirms that even under the conditions of the Nazi dictatorship and the Second World War, individuals still had some leeway and options to help protect people suffering persecution from mortal danger.

The exhibition centers on a media table on the main level, which is dedicated to eighteen subject areas. On the upper level, nine showcases document individual histories, each one introduced by a short film. Objects, documents, and photographs illustrate both successful and failed rescue attempts from the dual perspective of helpers and those who were rescued. An additional room is available for intensive research at computer terminals, with a database containing several hundred rescuers and those who were helped. Names are continually being added to this database.

The permanent exhibition is currently devoted to rescue attempts in Germany and the German-occupied territories. In a later phase it will be expanded to cover the European dimension as well. The preparations necessary for this expanded presentation will be implemented in the coming years, together with the Israeli Holocaust memorial Yad Vashem and European partner institutions.

Index of Names

Rentsch, Klara 49
Rentsch, Margarete 21
Rentsch, Paul 21, 22
Rewald, Ilse 69, 70
Rewald, Werner 69, 70
Richter, Herbert 21, 22
Richter, Maria 21
Ritzi, Wilhelm 29
Rosenthal, Fritz 77
Rosenthal, Hilde 77, 78
Rozenek, Jurek 61, 62
Rozenek, Michael 61, 62
Rutenborn, Angelika 81
Rutenborn, Günther 81
Saefkow, Anton 73, 74
Scharf, Erna 109, 110
Scharff, Werner 85, 86
Scheven, Elisabeth von 21, 22
Scheven, Walter von 21
Schindler, Emilie 97, 98
Schindler, Oskar 97, 98
Schmidt, Walter 89
Schmitz, Elisabeth 5, 13
Schneider, Gesine 18
Schneider, Hans-Reinhold 18
Schneider, Hildegard 18
Schneider, Jens 18
Schneider, Ruth 73
Schönhaus, Boris 105
Schönhaus, Cioma 105, 106
Schönhaus, Fanja 105
Schröder, Cornelia 70
Schröder, Hanning 70
Schröder, Nele 70
Schulz, Käthe 73
Schwarz, Evelyne 18
Schwerin, Ernst 45
Seibler, Else 73, 74
Siemsen, Gertie 17
Sommer, Margarete 5, 6
Spiegler, Zygmunt 53
Stadtler, Eduard 65
Stappenbeck, Hanna 21
Steffen, Elise 65
Steffen, Georg 65, 66
Stern, Izak 98
Stoltenhoff, Mathilde 65
Strauss, Ferdinand 101, 102
Strauss, Herbert 29, 45
Strauss, Lotte 29, 30, 45
Suhr, Otto 65
Suhr, Susanne 65
Süssmann, Brigitte 89, 90
Süssmann, Ruth 89, 90
Sussmann, Martha 89
Teves, Alfred 49
Themal, Rolf 90
Veit, Arthur 65, 66
Viere, Alfred 89
Viere, Martha 89, 90
Vorwalder, Willy 29
Waider, Hans 33
Wendland, Agnes 17, 81, 82
Wendland, Arndt 81
Wendland, Ruth 81, 82
Wendland, Walter 81
Wesslén, Erik 93
Wetzstein, Hugo 29
Winkler, Frida 85, 86
Winkler, Hans 85, 86
Wolff, Agnes 22
Wolff, Heinz Günther 21, 22
Wolzenburg, Fritz 69, 70
Zerna, Herta 66

Bibliography

Benz, Wolfgang, ed. *Überleben im Dritten Reich: Juden im Untergrund und ihre Helfer*. Munich: C. H. Beck, 2003

——, ed. *Solidarität und Hilfe für Juden während der NS-Zeit*. 7 vols. Berlin: Metropol, 1996–2004

Boehm, Eric H. *We Survived: Fourteen Histories of the Hidden and Hunted of Nazi Germany*. Revised and updated. Boulder, CO: Westview Press, 2003

Deutschkron, Inge. *Sie blieben im Schatten: Ein Denkmal für "stille Helden"*. Berlin: Hentrich, 1996

Fogelman, Eva. *Wir waren keine Helden: Lebensretter im Angesicht des Holocaust; Motive, Geschichten, Hintergründe*. Frankfurt and New York: Campus, 1995

Ginzel, Günther B., ed. *Mut zur Menschlichkeit: Hilfe für Verfolgte während der NS-Zeit*. Cologne: Rheinland, 1993

——, ed. *"... Das durfte keiner wissen!" Hilfe für Verfolgte im Rheinland von 1933 bis 1945; Gespräche, Dokumente, Texte*. Cologne: Rheinland, 1995

Grossmann, Kurt R. *Die unbesungenen Helden: Menschen in Deutschlands dunklen Tagen*. 2nd ed., revised and expanded. Frankfurt: Ullstein, 1984

Gutman, Israel (editor-in-chief), and Sara Bender (associate ed.). *Lexikon der Gerechten unter den Völkern: Deutsche und Österreicher*. With Daniel Fraenkel (German section editor) and Jakob Borut (Austrian section editor). Göttingen: Wallstein, 2005

——, eds. *The Encyclopedia of the Righteous Among the Nations: Europe (Part I) and Other Countries; Rescuers of Jews during the Holocaust*. Jerusalem: Yad Vashem, 2007

Kaplan, Marion. *Der Mut zum Überleben: Jüdische Frauen und ihre Familien in Nazideutschland*. Berlin: Aufbau Taschenbuch, 2003

Keim, Anton Maria, ed. *Die Judenretter aus Deutschland*. Mainz: Grünewald, 1983

Kosmala, Beate. "Zwischen Ahnen und Wissen: Flucht vor der Deportation (1941–1943)." In *Die Deportation der Juden aus Deutschland: Pläne—Praxis—Reaktionen 1938–1945* (Beiträge zur Geschichte des Nationalsozialismus, vol. 20), edited by Birthe Kundrus and Beate Meyer, 135–159. Göttingen: Wallstein, 2004

——, and Revital Ludewig-Kedmi. *Verbotene Hilfe: Deutsche Retterinnen und Retter während des Holocaust*, with a foreword by Emil Walter-Busch. Zurich: Pestalozzianum, 2003

——, and Claudia Schoppmann, eds. *Überleben im Untergrund: Hilfe für Juden in Deutschland 1941–1945*. Solidarität und Hilfe, vol. 5. Berlin: Metropol, 2002

——, eds. *Sie blieben unsichtbar: Zeugnisse aus den Jahren 1941 bis 1945*. Berlin: Förderverein Blindes Vertrauen, 2006

KWIET, KONRAD, and HELMUT ESCHWEGE. *Selbstbehauptung und Widerstand: Deutsche Juden im Kampf um Existenz und Menschenwürde 1933–1945.*
     Hamburg: Christians, 1984

LEUNER, HEINZ DAVID. *Gerettet vor dem Holocaust: Menschen, die halfen.* Frankfurt: Ullstein, 1989

LÖHKEN, WILFRIED, and WERNER VATHKE, eds. *Juden im Widerstand: Drei Gruppen zwischen Überlebenskampf und politischer Aktion Berlin 1939–1945.*
     Berlin: Edition Hentrich, 1993

RAU, JOHANNES, ed. *Hilfe für Verfolgte in der NS-Zeit: Jugendliche forschen vor Ort.* Hamburg: Edition Körber-Stiftung, 2002

RIFFEL, DENNIS. *Unbesungene Helden: Die Ehrungsinitiative des Berliner Senats 1958 bis 1966.* Berlin: Metropol, 2007

RÖHM, EBERHARD, and JÖRG THIERFELDER. *Juden—Christen—Deutsche 1933–1945.* Vols. 1–4. Stuttgart: Calwer, 1990–2007

RUDOLPH, KATRIN. *Hilfe beim Sprung ins Nichts: Franz Kaufmann und die Rettung von Juden und "nichtarischen" Christen.* Berlin: Metropol, 2005

SCHIEB, BARBARA, and MARTINA VOIGT. "Der Widerstand der Ohnmächtigen: Untergetauchte Juden und ihre Helfer in der NS-Zeit."
     Neue Gesellschaft/Frankfurter Hefte 2 (1998): 163–167

SCHIEB-SAMIZADEH, BARBARA. "Die kleinen Schritte der Forschung: Über die Schwierigkeiten, die Geschichte der Helfer der während der NS-Zeit
     versteckten Juden zu recherchieren." *Zeitgeschichte* 17, no. 11/12 (1990): 419–431

SCHOPPMANN, CLAUDIA. "Die 'Fabrikaktion' in Berlin: Hilfe für untergetauchte Juden als Form humanitären Widerstandes."
     Zeitschrift für Geschichtswissenschaft 2 (2005): 138–148

TAUSENDFREUND, DORIS. *Erzwungener Verrat: Jüdische "Greifer" im Dienst der Gestapo 1943–1945.* Berlin: Metropol, 2006

TUCHEL, JOHANNES, ed. *Der vergessene Widerstand: Zu Realgeschichte und Wahrnehmung des Kampfes gegen die NS-Diktatur.*
     Göttingen: Wallstein, 2005

WETTE, WOLFRAM, ed. *Stille Helden: Judenretter im Dreiländereck während des Zweiten Weltkriegs.* Freiburg im Breisgau: Herder, 2005

——, ed. *Retter in Uniform: Handlungsspielräume im Vernichtungskrieg der Wehrmacht.* Frankfurt: Fischer, 2002

——, ed. *Zivilcourage: Empörte Helfer und Retter aus Wehrmacht, Polizei und SS.* Frankfurt: Fischer, 2003

Acknowledgements

We would like to express our thanks for the many forms of support

Ruth Abraham	Pia Beyer	Edith Dietz	Helga Franke-Poelchau
Alice Ammermann	Henryk Birnbach	Jürgen Dittmer	Eberhard Fricke
Jochen Arndt	Jürgen Bogdahn	Nicole Dominicus	Margot Friedlander
Hildegard Arnold	Petra Bonavita	Käthe Drexler	Karin Friedrich
Dorothea Arnold-Theloe	Maria and Achim von Borries	Ruth Drossel	Wolfgang Friedrich
Zvi Aviram	Monika Breger	Eva Dunzendorfer	Eva Furth
Henry Bach	Henning von Brockdorff	Corinna Eichhorn	Arje Gaddai
Samuel Bak	Jutta and Klaus Bunke	Volker Eichler	Manfred Gailus
Kristiane Balogh-Keller	Günther Burckhardt	Gertrud Eisele	Adelheid Gehringer
Friederike Barkow	Lieselotte Collm	Andrea Engen	Carola Gerlach
Ben Barkow	William Cook	Isabel Enzenbach	Axel Gesch
Juliane and Michael von Barkow	Hanna Cooper	Lucia Euringer	Heiner Gölz
Daniel Barok	Maurice de Coulon	Zipora and Kalmi Eventov	Frank Görlich
Ulrich Baumann	Lother Czoßek	Günther and Lothar Fabian	Ester Golan
Peter Beier	Margarete Daene	Gisela Faust	Regina Goldmann
Peter Beisler	Lara Dämmig	Susanne Fetzer	Rolf Goldschagg
Berthold Beitz	Ditmar Danelius	Hans-Joachim Fliedner	Michael Good
Ursula Benjamin	Renate Danelius	Bernd Florath	Gerald von Gostomski
Wolfgang Benz	Karin Dengler	Christoph Foerster	Alfred Gottwaldt
Claus Bernet	Klaus Dettmer	Ernest Fontheim	Hellmut Griesmann
Madeleine von Bernstorff	Inge Deutschkron	Ernst Fraenkel	Evelyn Grollke
Heidi Bessler-Westrick	Klara Deutschländer-Furth	Leonie and Walter Frankenstein	Jan Groscurth

Wolf Gruner	Akim Jah	Marie-Luise Kreuter	Gerhard Lüdecke
Andreas Grunwald	Christine Jannasch	Christoph Kreutzmüller	Revital Ludewig-Kedmi
Ruth Gumpel	Manfred Joachim	Sabine Krusen	Hartmut Ludwig
Lili Haber	Walter Joelson	Gisela Kuck	Kay Lutze
Devorah Haberfeld	Hermann Jung	Stephan Kühmayer	Hans Madsen
Peter Haberkorn	Karen Jungblut	Ruth Kühne-Winkler	Marco Majoleth
Wolfgang Hammerschmidt	Eugen Kahl	Henriette Labbé	Simon Malkes
Maria Harms	Jutta Kauffmann	Gerlind Lachenicht	Maria Gräfin von Maltzan
Anita Heiliger	Christine Keck	Peter Lachmund	Antje Märke
Ernst Ludwig Heilmann	Rose Kessler	Inge Lammel	Gabi Marston
Peter Heilmann	Hermann Kimmich	Ellen and Konrad Latte	Frank Mecklenburg
Klaus Hellige	Renate and Jans Kingma	Karl-Heinz Lehmann	Eberhard Meier
Erika and Rolf Hensel	Heidi Kliem	Gerhard Lehmbruch	Ralf Melzer
Thomas Heppener	Wolf-Rüdiger Klisch	Jana Leichsenring	Helga Mesecke
Andreas Herbst	Ulrich Klopsch	Christel Leisering	Dora Metzger
Mathilde Herbst	Ken Knight	Dieter Lent	Lore Metzger
Christina Herkommer	Albert Knoll	Fred Lesniewski	Beate Meyer
Eugen Herman-Friede	Heinz Knapp	Esther Linde	Dietgard Meyer
Nele Hertling	Ruth Knoop	Jürgen Lindner	Kathrin Meyer
Josef Höfler	Annelise Kochmann	Georg Lippmann	Lutz Mez
Helga Isvoranu	Hannelore König	Stefan Litt	Franz and Peter Michalski
Gisela Jacobius	Werner König	Ilse Loewenberg	Siegfried Mielke
Helene Jacobs	Jackie Kohnstamm	Peter Loewenberg	Charles Milford
Andreas Jaffé	Marianne Krautzberger	Barbara Lovenheim	Andreas Mix

Vera Mölbitz	Cilli Plesser	Hans-Peter Ruess	Gesine Schwan
Frieder Mörike	Harald Poelchau jr.	Dietrich Ruge	Jizchak Schwersenz
Ulrike Moest	Heinz Putzrath	Karl E. Ruge	Stephan Sharf
Jörg Müller	Nanna Qvam	Angelika Rutenborn	Sara Shor
Wolfgang Müller	Christel Raack	Esther Sabelus	Patrick Siegele
Gaby Müller-Oelrichs	Jens Radtke	Rita Sakalis	Andrea Siemsen
Michael Müller-Stüler	Dietrich Raetzer	Lawrence Salinger	Ilona Simon Strimber
Günter Naumann	Michael Rainer	Hans-Rainer Sandvoß	Benno Simoni
Michael Naumann	Gary Ramm	Horst Sassin	Birgitta Skiba
Marion Neiss	Rolf Ramm	Werner Schallschmidt	Hannelore Skroblies
Kersti Nellberg	Stefan Reiß	Simone Scharbert	Hanna Sohst
Peter Neuhof	Elisabeth Reimer	Regina Scheer	Reha Sokolow
Ralph Neuman	Matthias Rentsch	Kurt Schilde	Jörg Thierfelder
Eva Nickel	Sabine Rentsch	Bernd Schmalhausen	Eugen Solf
Anette Nimmich	Ilse and Werner Rewald	Cornelia Schmalz-Jacobsen	Gertrud Solomon
Hanni Nörper	Thomas Richert	Margrit Schmidt	Hans-Ulrich Spieth
Cornelia Nowak	Detlev Riemer	Monika Schmidt	Christa Springe
Cord Pagenstecher	Dennis Riffel	Cioma Schönhaus	Georg Steffen
Mordecai Paldiel	Deborah Rimle Wolfson	Herbert Schrödter	Ulrich Steffen
Hanna Papanek	Elisabeth Ritzi-Gmür	Diana Schulle	Peter Steinbach
Haviva Peled-Carmeli	Erika Rode	Dagmar Schulz	Irena Steinfeldt
Mieczysław (Mietek) Pemper	Rita Rozenek	Elisabeth Schulz	Ute Stiepani
Johan Perwe	Katrin Rudolph	Sigrid Schulze	Ruth Stöffler
Joachim Piper	Elsa Ruess	Roswitha Schure	Constanze Stotz

126 ACKNOWLEDGEMENTS

Ingrid Strauch

Lotte and Herbert A. Strauss

Manfred Struck

Ruth Struwe

Horst Symanowski

Fred Taucher

Doris Tausendfreund

Ursula Timm

Volker Troche

Elisabeth Vollert

Jutta Wagner

Emil Walter-Busch

Manfred Warnecke

Rudolf Weckerling

Ruth Wedel

Henryk Weiffenbach

Elana Weiser

Clemens Weiss

Jutta Weitz

Barbara Welker

Bianca Welzing-Bräutigam

Konrad and Ludger Westrick

Wolfram Wette

Martin Widmann

Peter Widmann

Ruth Winkelmann

Hans Winter

Gisela and Gerhard Wittkowski

Dagmar Wittmers

Margot Wolf

Erika Wolff

Gerda Wolzenburg

Evelyn Woods

Hans M. Wuerth

Herta Zerna

Helga Zetzsche

Gerda Zorn

Anne-Frank-Zentrum

Archiv der Schwedischen Victoria-Gemeinde

Archiv der Technischen Universität Darmstadt

Archiv des Zentrums für Antisemitismusforschung
     der Technischen Universität Berlin

Bayerisches Hauptstaatsarchiv

Brandenburgisches Landeshauptarchiv

Bundesarchiv

Central Zionist Archives

Die Bundesbeauftrage für die Unterlagen des
     Staatssicherheitsdienstes der ehemaligen DDR

Deutsche Dienststelle (WASt)

Deutscher Caritasverband e.V.

Evangelische Kirchengemeinde Berlin-Kaulsdorf

Evangelisches Landeskirchliches Archiv in Berlin

Evangelisches Zentralarchiv Berlin

Förderverein Blindes Vertrauen e.V.

Fortunoff Video Archive for Holocaust Testimonies, Yale University

Freie Universität Berlin, Visual History Archive

Geheimes Staatsarchiv Preußischer Kulturbesitz

Geschichtswerkstatt Darmstadt

Heimatmuseum Berlin-Treptow

Institut Kirche und Judentum an der Humboldt-Universität zu Berlin

Institut für Zeitgeschichte

Internationaler Suchdienst (ITS)

Jüdisches Museum Berlin

Landesamt für Bürger- und Ordnungsangelegenheiten, Berlin,
Einwohnermeldeamt und Entschädigungsbehörde

Landesarchiv Berlin

Landeskirchliches Archiv Karlsruhe

Leo Baeck Institute

Mitte Museum Berlin

Museum Neukölln

Ölbaum Verlag

Pelikan GmbH

Prenzlauer Berg Museum

Robert-Havemann-Gesellschaft

H. Schmincke & Co.

Schweizerisches Bundesarchiv

Stadtarchiv Mannheim

Stiftung Denkmal für die ermordeten Juden Europas

Stiftung Neue Synagoge Berlin – Centrum Judaicum

Thüringisches Hauptstaatsarchiv

United States Holocaust Memorial Museum

Universitätsarchiv der Freien Universität Berlin

Universitätsarchiv der Humboldt-Universität Berlin

Universitätsarchiv der Ruprecht-Karls-Universität Heidelberg

University of Southern California, Shoah Foundation Institute for
Visual History and Education

Wichern-Verlag

Wisconsin Historical Society

Yad Vashem, The Holocaust Martyrs' and Heroes' Remembrance
Authority

Zentrum für Antisemitismusforschung

Photo Credits

Archiv des deutschen Caritasverbandes, Freiburg i. Br. page 4 left

Bundesarchiv page 20 right

Gedenkstätte Deutscher Widerstand, Berlin page 68

Institut für Zeitgeschichte, Munich page 16

Landesamt für Bürger- und Ordnungsangelegenheiten, Abt. I, Entschädigungsbehörde, Berlin page 11

From private collections pages 4 right, 8, 12, 15, 19, 23, 24, 27, 28, 35, 36, 39, 40, 43, 44, 47, 48, 51, 52, 55, 56, 59, 60, 63, 64, 67, 71, 72, 75, 76 left, 79, 80, 83, 84, 87, 88, 91, 92, 95, 99 right, 100, 104, 107, 108, 111

Robert-Havemann-Gesellschaft, Berlin page 20 left

Schweizerisches Bundesarchiv, Bern pages 31, 32, 103

Stadtarchiv Mannheim page 76 right

Thomas Bruns, photography pages 112, 115, 116, 117

United States Holocaust Memorial Museum, Washington D.C. page 99 left

    The views or opinions expressed in this exhibition and this book, and the context in which the image is used, do not necessarily reflect the views or policy of, nor imply approval or endorsement by The United States Holocaust Memorial Museum.

Yad Vashem, The Holocaust Martyrs' and Heroes' Remembrance Authority, Jerusalem page 96

Credits

PERMANENT EXHIBITION Silent Heroes: Resistance to Persecution of the Jews, 1933–1945.

A Documentation of the German Resistance Memorial Center Foundation, Silent Heroes Memorial Center, Rosenthaler Straße 39, D-10178 Berlin

PROJECT LEADERSHIP Prof. Dr. Johannes Tuchel

CONCEPT, EDITING, TEXTS Dr. Beate Kosmala | Barbara Schieb | Dr. Claudia Schoppmann | Prof. Dr. Johannes Tuchel | Martina Voigt
ASSISTANCE Karoline Georg | Taina Sivonen COORDINATION Susanne Brömel ENGLISH TRANSLATION AND EDITING Allison Brown

INTERIOR ARCHITECTURE, EXHIBITION DESIGN, OVERALL ARTISTIC DIRECTION Dorothée Hauck ASSISTANCE Markus Busch | Noel Nasir

MEDIA CONCEPTION AND PRODUCTION Lehmann & Werder Museumsmedien GbR ASSISTANCE à la prima grafikdesign | binaerpark GbR |
René Engelmann TECHNICAL MEDIA REALIZATION heddier electronic GmbH AUDIO PRODUCTION tonwelt professional media GmbH
SPEAKERS Marina Behnke | Christa Lewis | Clayton Nemrow | Marty Sander | Viola Sauer | Paul Sonderegger

LIGHT PLANNING XX Light, Olaf Adam EXHIBITION GRAPHICS M2M EXHIBITION PRINTS AND IMAGE PROCESSING Thomas Bruns, photography
FACSIMILES Susanne Jaeger, Grafik und Trick HISTORICAL RESTORATION OF WALL FINISHES IN STAIRWELL Sigrid Markiton, Farb- und Wandgestaltung

EXHIBITION FURNITURE Idaho Möbelbau EXHIBITION SPACE DESIGN Alois Albert (Planning), Siegl & Albert Bürogemeinschaft | Patricia Vacano
(Construction Site Management), Siegl & Albert Bürogemeinschaft | Sabine Benkwitz (Coordination), Stiftung Sozialpädagogisches Institut Berlin
"Walter May," Geschäftsbereich Stadtentwicklung, Ausnahme & Regel | Garrelt Hermanussen (Consulting Engineer and Wood Expert)
SHOWCASE ARRANGEMENT Abrell & van den Berg Ausstellungsservice GbR

CATALOG Silent Heroes Memorial Center

PUBLISHER Silent Heroes Memorial Center of the German Resistance Memorial Center Foundation

EDITORIAL DIRECTOR Prof. Dr. Johannes Tuchel

TEXTS Dr. Beate Kosmala | Barbara Schieb | Dr. Claudia Schoppmann | Prof. Dr. Johannes Tuchel | Martina Voigt

ENGLISH TRANSLATION Allison Brown

ENGLISH EDITING Ginger A. Diekmann

GRAPHIC DESIGN butscheidtplatz

OVERALL PRODUCTION Mercedes Druck

First English ed., translation of the 2nd, revised German ed., Berlin 2010

ISBN 978-3-926082-41-1

The German National Library (DNB) lists this publication in the German National Bibliography.
For detailed bibliographic data online, go to: http://dnb.d-nb.de

The Silent Heroes Memorial Center of the German Resistance Memorial Center Foundation is continuing to collect reports, photographs, and documents, and to archive video and audio recordings of oral history accounts of events.

CONTACTS

Dr. Beate Kosmala | Gedenkstätte Stille Helden, Rosenthaler Straße 39, D-10178 Berlin
TELEPHONE +49(0)30 23 45 79-19 FAX +49(0)30 23 45 79-39 E-MAIL kosmala@gdw-berlin.de

Barbara Schieb | Gedenkstätte Stille Helden, Rosenthaler Straße 39, D-10178 Berlin
TELEPHONE +49(0)30 23 45 79-29 FAX +49(0)30 23 45 79-39 E-MAIL schieb@gdw-berlin.de

www.gedenkstaette-stille-helden.de

132

Gedenkstätte
Deutscher Widerstand

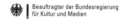

Beauftragter der Bundesregierung
für Kultur und Medien

Financed by the Federal Government
Commissioner for Culture and the Media
on the basis of a parliamentary resolution

EFRE

The exhibition and the catalog received funding from the Federal Government Commissioner for Culture and the Media and were co-financed by the European Union, European Regional Development Fund (ERDF), and the state of Berlin.